Japanese for Communication:
A Teacher's Guide

Paul Sandrock
Consultant
Foreign Language Education

Hisako Yoshiki
Consultant
Japanese Language Education

Wisconsin Department of Public Instruction
Madison, Wisconsin

This publication is available from

Publication Sales
Wisconsin Department of Public Instruction
Drawer 179
Milwaukee, WI 53293-0179
(800) 243-8782

Bulletin No. 96186

ISBN 1-57337-023-1

Printed on recycled paper.

Contents of the Guide

I am proud to present *Japanese for Communication: A Teacher's Guide*. Above all, this guide provides a thoughtful and thorough model for curriculum development that is adaptable to the wide variety of Japanese language programs in Wisconsin and around the world. Beginning with the publication in 1985 of the Department of Public Instruction's (DPI) *Guide to Curriculum Planning in Foreign Language*, Wisconsin has advocated an approach that emphasizes student proficiency in using a foreign language instead of simply being able to talk about the language. This guide will help teachers of Japanese envision how to implement such an approach in their classrooms.

This curriculum also forms the basis for future teacher development. Both preservice and inservice staff development will relate to implementing the vision for Japanese language education embodied in *Japanese for Communication*. University teacher-preparation programs can use this guide to inform future teachers about curriculum goals, instructional strategies, and suggested methods of assessment. It is my hope that this guide will serve as a valuable resource for future professional development workshops, courses, and conferences in order to continue the discussion and consensus-building that has begun through the development of this guide.

The DPI is very grateful to the Japan Foundation for providing Wisconsin with the services and expertise of Ms. Hisako Yoshiki, Japanese language advisor of the Japan Foundation. Ms. Yoshiki brings to Wisconsin her years of experience teaching Japanese and assisting teachers internationally. Ms. Yoshiki has worked with the developers of the guide since 1994, lending her knowledge and collaborating with Wisconsin's teachers both to gather ideas and to begin the implementation training.

A special thank you goes to the Japan Forum for joining the DPI as partners by generously funding the development of this guide. We are grateful for the support the Japan Forum has given to Wisconsin's teachers of Japanese.

John T. Benson
State Superintendent

Many educators worked faithfully over the past three years to develop the ideas embodied in this guide, to struggle over numerous pedagogical and philosophical issues, and to publish this curriculum. Though not listed by name, teachers involved in various DPI workshops suggested actual instruction and assessment activities that proved very helpful to the project. The authors wish to thank everyone involved.

Publications Task Force

This core group of educators was involved in development of all phases of the project.

Helena Curtain
Special Advisor to the Project
Foreign Language Curriculum Specialist
Milwaukee Public Schools

Pamela Delfosse
Teacher of Japanese, grades 9-12
Madison West High School

Diane Gulbronson
Teacher of Japanese, grades 9-12
New Berlin High Schools

Junko Mori
Lecturer in Japanese
Ph.D. candidate in Japanese linguistics
University of Wisconsin-Madison
Former intern at a Wisconsin high school
Japanese Language and Culture
    Assistants Program (JALCAP)

Kazuko Stone
Teacher of Japanese, grades K-12
Green Bay Public Schools

Contributors

The task force was initially assisted by the following educators:

Yukio Itoh
Former Wisconsin teacher of
Japanese, grades 9-12
The Japan Forum

Andrea Waxman
Teacher of Japanese, grades 9-12
Wauwatosa School District

Steve Webb
Teacher of Japanese, grades 9-12
Denmark High School

Ken White
Professor of Japanese
Beloit College

Reviewers

These teachers served as reviewers, shared ideas, and piloted the ideas in curriculum units.

Jaci Collins
Teacher of Japanese, grades 7-12
Manitowoc Public Schools

Peggy Hagmann
Teacher of Japanese, grades 9-12
Eau Claire North High School

Penny Mertz
Teacher of Japanese, grades 7-12
Northeast Wisconsin Telecommunications
Education Consortium

Gloria Rozmus
Teacher of Japanese, grades 7-12
Menomonee Falls Schools

Lynn Sessler Schmaling
Teacher of Japanese, grades K-2 and 9-12
Menasha Public Schools

Akiko Uchiyama
Teacher of Japanese, grades 7-12
Greenfield Public Schools

Additional assistance was provided by the following:

Elizabeth Borstad
Teacher of Japanese, grades 7-12
St. Francis Public Schools

Gary St. Clair
Teacher of Japanese, grades 9-12
Sheboygan Lutheran High School

Kiku Harvey
Teacher of Japanese, grades 6-8
Wauwatosa School District

Teruhiko Oshima
Teaching Assistant
Japanese Language Exchange Program
(JALEX)
Walker Middle School, Milwaukee

Staff Contributors

Division for Learning Support: Instructional Services

Pauline M. Nikolay
Assistant State Superintendent

Tom Stefonek
Division-wide Director, Budget and Data Management

Susan Grady
Education Program Coordinator

Connie Haas
Program Assistant

Peggy Solberg
Program Assistant

Division for Libraries and Community Learning

Publications and Media Services
Yoko Oyamada, Text Editor
Brian Satrom, Text Editor
Michael V. Uschan, Proofreader
Victoria Horn, Graphic Artist
Kathy Addie, Management Information Technician
Heather Lins, Management Information Technician

The authors would especially like to thank the Japan Forum, Tokyo, for generously funding *Japanese for Communication: A Teacher's Guide* and the Japan Foundation Language Center, Santa Monica, California, and its staff for the collaboration and encouragement it provided.

Also, thank you to the Japanese Language Exchange Program teaching assistants, who regularly assisted Wisconsin teachers of Japanese in all aspects of this project.

This document is still a work in progress. The authors are glad to put this framework into teachers' hands, and desire feedback as schools pilot the curriculum.

x

Rationale 1

Japanese as an International Language

At the same time that they use Japanese to communicate on a full range of topics, students should learn the unique perspectives of the Japanese people as they practice the use of language in culture.

This curriculum will help students use Japanese to talk about meaningful issues. Increasingly, teachers of Japanese are recognizing that the Japanese language is no longer limited to Japanese culture but is becoming a means of communication in an international community. To reflect the needs of learners and the fact that most U. S. students will not use Japanese to live in Japan, this guide is designed to teach Japanese as a foreign language outside Japan, not as a second language taught in Japan.

At the same time that they use Japanese to communicate on a full range of topics, students should learn the unique perspectives of the Japanese people as they practice the use of language *in* culture. Two principles are critical to this curriculum:

- Japanese may be used as a tool for communication anywhere in the world with people of different cultural backgrounds. Given such a context, instruction should focus more on the meaning being expressed than on cultural restrictions in language usage, such as the correct use of honorifics.
- In order to reach higher levels of proficiency, students need to develop a sociolinguistic competence to be able to use Japanese correctly within Japanese culture. The goal is to enable students to behave in a socially appropriate manner when in contact with Japanese people in their settings.

Combining these two principles, the teacher will have a more tolerant attitude toward beginning students' attempts at communication while introducing students to the sociolinguistic competence that is critical to improved use of the language.

In developing this guide, key questions were, Why study only one culture? Why study a cultural phenomenon from only one viewpoint? This curriculum should allow students to use Japanese to explore themes from a view wider than that of a single culture but also to understand the Japanese view of those themes (National Standards, 1996). For example, students may explore the concept of family from many cultural perspectives through the medium of the Japanese language while simultaneously gaining insights about Japanese families, information that is usually not available in other classes.

Broad Goals

With these points in mind, this curriculum is guided by the following broad goals. These goals are addressed to the student to establish what he or she should know and be able to do as a result of instruction based on this curriculum.

Develop a Personal Rationale for Learning the Japanese Language and Culture

- Express the value of knowing Japanese language and culture.
- Develop effective language-learning strategies.
- Show effort to apply beyond the classroom what is learned.
- Examine cultural stereotypes.
- Explore similarities between Japanese and U.S. cultures.
- Understand one's own culture by examining another culture.

Speak with Native Speakers in Increasingly Complex Situations

- Develop vocabulary and structures needed to communicate at various levels of complexity with the proper level of formality.
- Speak the language with accurate pronunciation and intonation so that it is comprehensible to native speakers.
- Understand and use nonverbal signals (body language).
- Recognize the existence of different levels of politeness.

Develop Reading and Writing Skills in Authentic Japanese from the Beginning of the Program

- Read and write *hiragana* and *katakana* characters directly, without the use of romanized writing.
- Recognize meaning of essential *kanji*.
— Focus on recognition over production.
— Learn *kanji* according to survival needs within content themes.
- Read to meet daily needs.
- Read for the main idea and, depending on language level, understand an increasing amount of detail.
— Skim for meaning at different levels.
— Perform appropriate tasks using authentic materials.
- From the beginning, learn basic writing conventions, such as stroke order, and horizontal and vertical writing formats.
- Write to express one's own ideas.
- Write with increasing attention to accuracy and with increasing complexity.

Survive in a Japanese Environment and Fulfill Basic Needs

- Purchase food.
- Function in shopping situations.
- Secure shelter.
- Use various means of transportation.
- Function in a classroom.
- Use Japanese for socialization.
- Understand and use language in emergencies.

Understand and Appreciate the Uniqueness of Japanese Culture

- Know and use culturally specific behaviors.
- Understand cultural background in the use of language.
- Demonstrate knowledge of basic geographical facts about Japan.
- Demonstrate knowledge of Japanese and Japanese-American contributions to art, literature, music, drama, and other fine arts, and their influence on Western culture.
- Be acquainted with significant events or stages of Japanese history.
- Be aware of the main religious and philosophical influences on Japan.
- Understand the political, sociological, technological, and educational aspects of contemporary Japan.

The Need for this Guide

Currently, enrollment for Japanese in Wisconsin's schools is growing at a faster rate than for any other language. In Wisconsin, a wide variety of Japanese language programs exist, as do teachers with widely varying backgrounds and preparation. These programs face several difficulties.

• Programs vary in the length and continuity of their instruction. Some programs offer kindergarten through twelfth grade instruction. Others offer instruction from grades 6-12, grades 9-12, or only two years of senior high school.

• Within some districts there has not always been a clear curriculum to connect pre-high school experiences to senior high courses.

• Textbooks and other resource materials are limited and vary in their quality and usefulness.

• An effective means of transition between secondary and university programs of Japanese does not yet exist.

The *Japanese for Communication* curriculum will help in addressing each of these difficulties by creating a consensus on what students will know and be able to do through a local district's program of Japanese instruction.

While this curriculum is an outgrowth of the current needs of Japanese programs in Wisconsin, it will also help other states that are at similar points in developing Japanese language instruction. The purpose of this guide is to provide these diverse programs with a cohesive framework and common goals.

Beyond providing a common framework for instruction and assessment, this guide will help teachers organize their own instruction.

Beyond providing a common framework for instruction and assessment, this guide will help teachers organize their own instruction. Typically, teachers let a textbook organize their instruction, allowing it to dictate the content of their teaching. Teachers using this guide, however, are no longer confined to their textbook or its sequential presentation of content. This guide's cohesive, yet flexible framework allows teachers to systematically incorporate content from their text and other resources, but these need not dominate or direct their course. This guide will enable teachers to make more conscious decisions regarding their curriculum, assessment, and instruction.

Philosophical Base of the Curriculum

The curriculum begins with clear statements of what students will be able to do with the language they are learning. These statements, or outcomes, show language in use. From these outcomes, examples of what a student might actually say have been generated. Finally, from these sample expressions, the inherent linguistic structures are identified. This order of development matches student motivation to learn a foreign language. In contrast, traditional curricula start with a prescribed sequence of language structures, generate sample expressions (often organized into unnatural dialogues), and finally declare what students should be able to do with language.

Developmental Language Levels

The curriculum is organized under four developmental language levels: beginning, transitional, intermediate, and advanced. These terms refer to program organization and curriculum organization. They do not correspond with the Proficiency Guidelines of the American Council on the Teaching of Foreign Languages (ACTFL) (1986). The terms have been chosen to avoid using numbers to label the levels, which would send the message that a developmental level is learned in a year of instruction. Experience indicates that students rarely accomplish what is described in a text for a level in one school year.

This guide is built on the principle that the language (vocabulary and structures) and context (themes) are reintroduced and practiced in new and more in-depth ways across language levels, with students able to demonstrate increasing understanding and fluency. Language acquisition is not a sequential process of mastering one piece of content before moving to another.

The broad objectives for each level are summarized as follows:

Beginning Level. The overall objective is to be able to discuss various topics from a personal perspective, participate in simple exchanges of information, describe basic elements of the theme under discussion, and use basic expressions in a culturally appropriate and socially polite manner.

Transitional Level. Characteristics include a beginning ability to manipulate the language elements that the student knows, to creatively use the language, to apply the language in less-controlled situations, to begin to describe cultural phenomena, and to begin to use language to express more original ideas, such as opinions and concerns.

Intermediate Level. The general objective is to show more manipulative control over the language, being able to deal with spontaneous changes, discuss issues (not just concrete situations), show more control and depth in narration, and show more originality in written expression.

Advanced Level. The broad objective is to carry on a discussion in depth and detail, express understanding of the form and substance of Japanese culture, function in a broad range of real situations encountered in Japan, persuade others, substantiate opinions, and hypothesize.

The expectation is that by completing this curriculum in a K-12 program, students will be able to reach an intermediate level of proficiency as described by the ACTFL proficiency guidelines.

Program Models and Adaptations

Consistency across a variety of programs is increased by the common vision, common goals, and common outcomes of this curriculum. Whether students experience some instruction in middle school, an immersion program in elementary school, or three years of regular instruction at a senior high school, they will be working toward the same goals and developing the same attitudes and skills. Students will not end up confused by one experience in *romaji*, another all in *hiragana*, and another with no attention to

By adapting this curriculum to the amount of time available for instruction, the various stages will connect and students will experience continuous progress along the continuum of proficiency.

writing. By adapting this curriculum to the amount of time available for instruction, the various stages will connect and students will experience continuous progress along the continuum of proficiency. As one example, the beginning stage could be the curriculum for a K-5 program, or for grades 6-8, or the basis for the course in grade 9 and part of 10.

The design of this curriculum will, therefore, support a variety of program models. The four language development stages might be adapted to K-12, 6-12, or 9-12 programs as shown in the following chart:

Level	K-12 Design	6-12 Design	9-12 Design
Beginning Level	Grades K-5	Grades 6-8	Grades 9-10
Transitional Level	6-8	9-10	10-11
Intermediate Level	9-10	10-11	11-12
Advanced Level	11-12	12-Postsecondary	Postsecondary

Such adaptability also allows students to begin the study of Japanese at various points in the school program. Because the focus is on what a student can do in the language, there is less specificity in which vocabulary a student must know. Rather than requiring a student to translate a set paragraph about school, the question to ask is, Can a student describe his or her school? If the student can do so, then he or she has accomplished the goal. The teacher does not have to force all students in a course to know exactly the same vocabulary as a prerequisite; the students should be able to function at a given level or stage by demonstrating their ability to use language within the functional range of that course.

Rather than requiring a student to translate a set paragraph about school, the question to ask is, Can a student describe his or her school?

Program Articulation

This curriculum can provide the start of a dialogue between university and K-12 programs, with the goal of informing university programs of what K-12 programs are able to teach. Hopefully this will insure smoother transitions for students from elementary through university instruction.

To ensure that this curriculum will provide substantive preparation for students who may want to continue their study of Japanese beyond their K-12 education, the structures and skills included in the curriculum were checked in several ways. Native speakers identified the structures included in the sample expressions that students will use to show achievement of the language outcomes. These structures were then compared to the contents of several pre-college and college level texts, and to the Japan Foundation Proficiency Test (levels 4 and 3). This comparison suggested that students who successfully complete the *Japanese for Communication* curriculum should qualify for a course more advanced than the initial university course in Japanese. University students in their first year of Japanese study may cover some items that will not be included in this curriculum; however, the depth of skill development should allow students who complete this curriculum to successfully function beyond a beginning course.

This guide advocates a longer period of exposure for so-called totally foreign languages, as is suggested in the National Foreign Language Center's *A Framework for Introductory Japanese Language Curricula in American High Schools and Colleges* (1993). Students in the U.S. bring little knowledge of or experience with Japanese culture to the Japanese language classroom. It is important to establish familiarity with the cultural background in order to successfully learn a foreign language.

The unfamiliarity with the language structure and writing system also means that learning Japanese will take longer. Students studying European languages for four "years" may reach higher levels of proficiency than students spending an equal time studying Japanese. The Foreign Service Institute (Omaggio, 1993) makes this point clear in its comparison of the time necessary to achieve a similar level of proficiency in various languages. Spanish and French are placed as Level I languages and Japanese as a Level IV language for U.S. senior high or university students. This means that U.S. students require 480 to 720 hours to reach the intermediate level of proficiency in Japanese compared to 240 hours to reach intermediate proficiency in French.

Therefore, beginning students need to spend more time in a recognition phase, but not to the exclusion of other skills. The question is one of emphasis, meaning that instruction with beginning students should focus more on listening and speaking but without neglecting beginning reading and writing.

Learning Japanese in the U.S.

Learning Japanese in the U.S. is different from learning Japanese in Japan. Some of the challenges to learning Japanese in the U.S. differing from those found in the more commonly taught languages, such as French, German, and Spanish, include the following:
• cognates that often are transformed beyond recognition.
• the complex cultural code embedded in the Japanese language, such as
— gender-specific speech.
— age-specific speech.
— honorifics based on hierarchy and the in-group/out-group concept.
• uniqueness of the Japanese writing system, including
— the use of three integrated nonalphabetic scripts.
— the need for training in handwriting.
• differences in the "skill mix" relationship of reading to listening and speaking, including
— the immense gap that exists between the spoken and the written language, compared to the direct relationship among listening, speaking, reading, and writing in European languages.
— the fact that reading comprehension of *kanji* does not guarantee oral production.
• the need for making technology available for students and teachers, such as computer programs to assist with writing.
• materials (texts and authentic materials) that often require adaptations to make them comprehensible to students.
• the need for materials and tasks that reflect the special interests of U.S. students.

Characteristics of Effective Foreign Language Instruction

Because of the uniqueness of the Japanese language, this curriculum also calls for a shift in the way that Japanese is taught. Proficiency-oriented instruction matches the philosophy behind this curriculum. The National Association of District Supervisors of Foreign Language (NADSFL) (1991) guidelines listed below, identifying characteristics of effective foreign language instruction, are a good summary of this philosophy. The guidelines provide a basis for common understanding and communication among evaluators, observers, and practitioners in foreign language classrooms. Because of the unique characteristics of Japanese, this guide has added some unique methodological considerations for teaching Japanese to the original NADSFL guidelines. These adaptations are printed in italics.

- The teacher uses the target language extensively, encouraging the students to do so. *The classroom atmosphere created by the teacher is crucial to encouraging student production of language (speaking and writing) as well as to developing comfort for student reception of language (listening and reading). This atmosphere is created when the teacher models authentic language from an advanced level of proficiency.*
- The teacher provides opportunities to communicate in the target language in meaningful, purposeful activities that simulate real-life situations. *The use of authentic materials, such as Japanese menus and train timetables, is both motivating, supportive of students unfamiliar with the language system, and suggestive of future applications.*
- Skill-getting activities enable students to participate successfully in skill-using activities. Skill-using activities predominate.
- Time devoted to listening, speaking, reading, and writing is appropriate to course objectives and to the language skills of the students.
- Culture is systematically incorporated into instruction.
- *Culture needs to be more broadly defined in the foreign language classroom to include not only the target culture, but also to involve the student in sharing and examining his or her own culture.*
- *In order to become proficient in using the Japanese language, students must acquire the Japanese culture as well. Language must be learned in its cultural context.*
- *In teaching culture, a balance between contemporary and traditional culture should be maintained.*
- *Brief culture capsules need to contain a language element, and language needs to be presented in its cultural context as much as possible.*
- The teacher uses a variety of student groupings.
- Most activities are student-centered.
- The teacher uses explicit error correction in activities which focus on accuracy, and implicit or no error correction in activities which focus on communication. *In both cases, broad program goals and expectations of specific activities must be clear to students.*
- Assessment, both formal and informal, reflects the way students are taught.
- Student tasks and teacher questions reflect a range of thinking skills.

- Instruction addresses student learning styles.
- Students are explicitly taught foreign language learning strategies and are encouraged to assess their own progress. *Such learning-to-learn skills provide students with a greater degree of independence.*
- The teacher enables all students to be successful. *High teacher expectations for all students are seen as a key to student success. The teacher provides opportunities for students to achieve the course goals.*
- The teacher establishes an affective climate in which students feel comfortable taking risks.
- Students are enabled to develop positive attitudes toward cultural diversity. *The goal is to recognize and understand cultural differences both inside as well as outside the school. Part of this goal is to develop conflict resolution skills.*
- The physical environment reflects the target language and culture.
- The teacher uses the textbook as a tool, not as curriculum.
- The teacher uses a variety of print and nonprint materials including authentic materials. *The presentation of authentic materials in Japanese poses a unique challenge. At times, simulated versions of authentic materials may be necessary to provide support to the beginning reader.*
- Technology, as available, is used to facilitate teaching and learning.
- The teacher engages in continued professional development in the areas of language skills, cultural knowledge, and current methodology.

Format of the Curriculum

The format is designed to establish a focus for instruction and learning. Rather than providing lists of structures and vocabulary to memorize, this curriculum sets clear goals for teachers to plan daily lessons and for students to chart progress toward proficiency. The guide identifies major themes to organize instruction and to provide a context for instruction. Specific outcomes describe what students will be able to do with Japanese at each developmental level. Assessment activities are suggested to illustrate each outcome. From this base of language in use, the curriculum provides sample expressions, their linguistic structures, and vocabulary to assist teachers in planning lessons.

Rather than providing lists of structures and vocabulary to memorize, this curriculum sets clear goals for teachers to plan daily lessons and for students to chart progress toward proficiency.

Instructional Themes

Themes provide an ongoing framework around which students develop their skill in using Japanese. The framework consists of 12 themes or meaningful content areas. Most textbooks and curricula treat themes as topics that are introduced and exhausted at one exposure in one year. This guide focuses on the continuous progress of students, purposefully repeating the thematic focus at each level of instruction. This allows students to review and then build on their prior knowledge within each theme. One example is to introduce vocabulary for the immediate family at the beginning level and then to expand the vocabulary to include extended family relationships at the transitional level.

Some themes may work well together, as when a teacher designs instruction to teach from two themes simultaneously. One such pairing could be Home and Community being taught with Self, Family, and Friends. Different combinations may seem appropriate at different levels.

Some themes are overarching and should not be taught in a single unit. Such themes work well and naturally together with other themes. The themes of Means of Communication and Japan and the World connect with other themes, and most logically will occur throughout the year. The outcomes of Means of Communication are more process-oriented and, therefore, could be met while focusing on the content under another theme. The outcomes of Japan and the World are also designed to be integrated with every teaching unit. Japan and the World is not a single unit to be taught and then set aside.

Expectations of what students should achieve in each theme increase as the outcomes and contexts are reintroduced from level to level. In the theme of Home and Community, for example, the context of "What housing exists in a neighborhood?" at the beginning level leads to the context of "What differences in housing can be attributed to geography?" at the transitional level and to the context of "How does a community change over time?" at the advanced level. Figure 1 provides a listing and description of the themes.

Outcomes

Outcomes are clear statements of what students should know and be able to do. Detailed outcomes are provided for each of the twelve themes for two to four levels. Because of the thematic organization of this guide, language functions (such as making a request) are not listed as a separate element. Rather, language functions are embedded in the outcomes. The guiding principles for choosing these outcomes are that the outcome is meaningful to students; represents an authentic, functional use *by students* of language; and can be assessed. The focus throughout this guide is on realistic, authentic situations. This desire is balanced with the motivation of being able to communicate similarly to one's functioning ability in English.

The focus throughout this guide is on realistic, authentic situations.

It is advisable to repeat outcomes either in the same theme, but at different levels, or in different themes. Vocabulary and, even more importantly, linguistic structures need to be reviewed throughout a program. The application of vocabulary and structures in other themes or wider contexts is a sign of increasing proficiency.

The outcomes correspond to the students' linguistic ability at each level. There is no prescribed number of outcomes per theme or level. From level to level, the outcomes ask the students to show higher levels of language proficiency. The teacher will clearly see the match of each outcome to suggested assessment activities and, further, to the context, sample expressions, and structures.

An outcome may actually be used as the basis for two or three groups of sample expressions. Some outcomes may be first expressed in listening and speaking terms and later be more closely linked to developing reading and writing skills. In such cases, a new set of expressions may not have been added.

Figure 1

Themes

Daily Routines—Two levels
Students learn to talk about their day-to-day lives and the cultural shaping of routines, such as meals, school routines, and use of free time. Students also use language to deal with changes in routines.

Home and Community—Four levels
Students focus on describing their home, neighborhood, and region. Issues to explore include the description and preservation of plants and animals in their natural environment, and how customs and attitudes change over time and across cultures.

Japan and the World—Four levels
This theme asks students to explore how cultures affect each other, including the sharing of words and customs, and how the past affects the present and future.

Leisure/Free Time—Four levels
Students discover similarities and differences in how young people use their free time around the world, how culture influences these choices, and how to perform various activities.

Means of Communication—Three levels
The focus in this theme is on using different means of communication, such as phones and answering machines, fax machines, e-mail, handwritten notes, and business cards. Students practice using active listening techniques and different writing styles matched to the purpose and the medium.

My Body/My Heath—Four levels
This theme includes using language to report feelings and emotions, as well as to learn about healthy habits and cultural influences in making choices.

Rites of Passage—Four levels
The context explored is important points of transition in a person's life, including such milestones as births, school graduations, permission to drive, employment, marriages, and funerals. Students use language to learn how these events are observed and how customs associated with such events change over time.

Schools and Education—Four levels
Students learn about the elements of school culture, how education is structured, and how to function in a school setting.

Seasonal Events—Three levels
In this theme, students understand and learn to participate in the various activities or celebrations that are associated with different seasons of the year.

Self, Family, and Friends—Four levels
Students learn to talk about and with family members and friends. They explore how different cultures define the range of what constitutes a family and the roles and responsibilities of different family members.

Shopping—Four levels
The context for practicing language skills under this theme is making purchases, the variety in stores, shopping habits and attitudes, and advertisements.

Travel and Transportation—Four levels
Students use language to travel for a wide variety of purposes, both day-to-day and recreational. This theme focuses on creating the attitude of an explorer rather than of a tourist.

The development of *kanji* is ongoing, so sometimes the recognition or production of *kanji* for a particular theme is listed as an outcome. This reinforces the importance of contextualized and appropriate assessment of *kanji*.

The outcomes will be realized through careful lesson planning, selection of appropriate methodology, and student involvement in learning. The level of specificity is sufficient for the teacher to envision various implementation ideas without being so specific as to produce only one possibility. Teachers should pick and choose the appropriate content for any given course, supplying detail as they see fit in order to help students achieve the detailed outcomes.

Suggested Assessment Activities

In order to clarify each outcome, an assessment activity is suggested (Brown, 1995). This gives the teacher a sense of what level of performance is expected of students to show successful achievement of the matched outcome. The outcome establishes what a student will be able to do; the assessment describes how and how well the student will demonstrate achievement of that outcome. An important aspect of assessment is that it gives the student a sense of what is valued in language learning. The description of the expected performance helps the teacher to plan the classroom instruction to lead to success in the assessment.

The assessments try to show the variety of ways in which assessment must take place in order to match various student learning styles. Assessment must go beyond paper and pencil tests or textbook-generated quizzes. The assessment activities incorporate use of listening, speaking, reading, writing, and culture skills. The goal is to blur the line between assessment and practice, encouraging teachers to look for opportunities for assessing students rather than relying only on formal test events. The suggested assessment activities may be viewed as examples of both teaching strategies and assessment strategies that will help a teacher to implement the *Japanese for Communication* curriculum.

Context

The context is best described as an area for exploration. The context provides a clearer focus for the teacher's lesson planning, helping teachers plan classroom activities. The context gives the teacher and students questions to investigate, thus embedding language functions in a cultural and situational context. Language becomes real and useful as they explore topics suggested in the context. Using the language through these questions, students should be able to show achievement of the outcomes for that theme at the given level. Sample expressions and vocabulary provide a more detailed look at how students will use language in each context.

Language must always be taught in a context, not in isolation (Omaggio, 1993). Foreign language educators have focused for too long only on teaching or testing the language pieces rather than employing them toward a larger purpose. Students start to connect language components through a meaningful context. Language outcomes are more generic; the context is more specific. The outcomes and pieces *alone* are not meaningful; the context connects them in a meaningful way. That context must come from a conscious decision that considers what is helpful, valuable, useful, and of interest to the student. Obviously, students functioning at a higher level of proficiency are able to go into more depth in a given content area. This is reflected in each theme through the increasing sophistication of the context from one level to the next.

Culture

The goal in teaching culture is to create empathy through shared experience. Instruction must focus on cultural similarities as much as cultural differences. The attitude to be developed is that of an explorer, not a tourist or traveler, in which students understand the "why" behind attitudes and actions within a culture.

The culture elements in this curriculum are not prescriptive, rather the goal is to teach culture study skills and attitudes. For this reason, this curriculum contains less cultural detail, such as a prescribed culture curriculum of *kimono, origami,* and *sushi.* At upper levels, students will understand such cultural phenomenon from a deeper level of knowledge through various experiences and exposures over the previous years of instruction. This curriculum stresses the importance of students learning to use the Japanese language by using it to discuss cultural themes that are more international than monoculturally specific. The danger in teaching only Japanese culture is that stereotypes may be reinforced.

The attitude to be developed is that of an explorer, not a tourist or traveler...

Culture is found in language; language infuses culture. Culture is not static but adapts and evolves. A prescriptive listing of culture would have several problems. Authentic culture is constantly changing, outdating any listing as it is published, and a listing could not be exhaustive nor responsive to the materials available to the teacher. Students need personal experiences to verify their increasing cultural knowledge, so lists of culture topics would not be appropriate in this framework. Some of the suggestions for appropriate cultural content surface in the suggested assessment activities and in the sample expressions. Even in the vocabulary section, certain topics of related culture become clear. Culture is embedded throughout *Japanese for Communication*, surfacing in the language usage and in the teaching through the context.

A goal of this curriculum is that teachers will examine what they teach to make sure that they are not reinforcing stereotypes. Often the decision on what aspects of culture to teach is a question of degrees. Taking off one's shoes on entering a home is still important to most Japanese. Ignorance of this could put the student in an awkward situation because this cultural phenomenon is tied to a value system that runs deeper than simple custom. However, wearing a mask in public to cover one's nose and mouth when suffering from a cold is not such a critical piece of culture to learn because it may be a changing attitude that cannot be dealt with as an absolute. Teachers need to examine their cultural content to decide the appropriate means of reaching the broad goals and objectives for each level. This curriculum provides a structure for the systematic presentation of a broad spectrum of cultural information and experiences.

Sample Expressions

In order to achieve the outcomes and to carry out the assessment activities, students need language components. These components consist of expressions and their corresponding structures. The expressions included in this curriculum are samples of the language a student might use to achieve each outcome.

As much as possible, the sample expressions represent authentic language, or what might naturally be said or written in the contextualized situation. Students will use expressions similar to these examples in order to demonstrate the outcomes for a theme at a certain level of language development. The expressions have been selected based on what situations U.S. students will encounter for using their Japanese. The expressions support and follow the order of the context.

Each expression is given in the formal style, which is the *desu/masu* form. For beginning students, the spoken and written forms learned will be the same. At more advanced levels, however, the distinctions among various registers of spoken and written language need to be introduced. Likewise, *kanji* are included in the way that they would naturally appear, not necessarily representing what students will write.

A similar consideration has been given to the level of honorifics to be included and to the degree this should be taught for U.S. students. For K-12 students, awareness and use of some levels of *keigo* is helpful, but study of the full range of uses is appropriate for later study. The goal in this curriculum is that students will feel comfortable using the appropriate *desu/masu* style and comprehending honorifics as specified in the outcomes of the themes. At the same time, as well as honorifics, teachers should consciously incorporate the less formal style used with family and peers as appropriate and necessary. To support this, some samples in the less formal style are provided in the resource section.

Sample expressions are handled at the sentence level, or in the form of a question and answer, or as a statement and response. These expressions can be adapted to other situations as students become comfortable using different vocabulary.

The list of sample expressions is not exhaustive. The teacher should select other expressions and structures of a similar level in order to create more comprehensive teaching units. To help the teacher make such choices, a more complete list of functions, related expressions, and their embedded structures is supplied in the resources section of this guide, including some expressions in a less formal style. Teachers need background knowledge to recognize the appropriate use of these less formal expressions by gender and age. Specialized knowledge is also needed to note the differences between oral and written language patterns. Teachers should use their own expertise to make decisions on teaching these formal expressions.

Structures

After providing sample expressions, this guide identifies the linguistic structures embedded in these expressions. A generic list in the resource section summarizes the breadth and depth of structures that are part of the curriculum. Through each theme, the structures are practiced across each level. This reassures the teacher that necessary elements of the language are being used and taught. The purpose of the sample expressions and structures is as much to help the teacher as to provide a vehicle for articulation.

Placing structures within the context of a theme insures that they are not taught in isolation or for their own sake. Structures are always a means to the end, which is communication. Structures are chosen on the basis of how they support the set outcomes. Structures are not taught at a single point in the curriculum, rather they are reintroduced throughout the themes at a given level and across the various levels in different themes. Students will show increasing sophistication and control in their use of structures over the course of the curriculum.

Structures are always a means to the end, which is communication.

Orthography

Proficiency in the use of *kanji* is an ongoing task. Throughout this curriculum, *kanji* are used in natural expressions. To emphasize the authentic nature of the expressions, *kanji* are not placed in an isolated list but incorporated into the vocabulary section at the end of each theme or within the sample expressions of each theme. Designating which *kanji* are to be introduced in which sequence would not fit the philosophy of this guide. The same *kanji* may appear at several different levels and in several different themes.

For this guide, *kanji* have not been selected from a predetermined list, since *kanji* must be learned in a context. The choices have been made on the basis of what students need to achieve the stated outcomes and to show an increasing level of proficiency. The *kanji* used are those needed for survival in communicating what is essential within the outcomes and the language context.

Teachers should not consider teaching every *kanji* by level as they appear in the sample expressions or vocabulary sections. Rather, the *kanji* shown give examples of how *kanji* are used. *Kanji* are sometimes listed as an outcome in order to give importance to assessing students' increasing control of *kanji*.

Since written Japanese is so complex (even for native Japanese who continue to learn new *kanji* through the twelfth grade), U.S. students should begin their study of orthography from the beginning level concurrently with the other skill areas.

Vocabulary

At the end of the descriptions of each theme, suggested vocabulary for the entire theme is provided as a resource for the teacher. The list provided is not prescriptive, but is a beginning to help the teacher in developing lesson plans. The selections are made to suggest some of the breadth and depth of content to be included within each theme in support of the language context.

Wisconsin teachers of Japanese contributed to the list by suggesting vocabulary they are using or want to know in order to use Japanese in the given theme. The vocabulary listed at the end of each theme is not designed to be a required list that students must memorize. Students will develop control over and memorize many of the words given; however, students are not expected to know all of them. A communicative curriculum allows student choice in vocabulary because the emphasis is on the student picking up the language tools needed to express his or her own thoughts.

Another criterion for selection of vocabulary for this listing is to provide words that are not easily available to non-native speakers, words not readily found in most bilingual dictionaries. Like culture, vocabulary needs constant updating. The vocabulary resource list will prove especially helpful to non-native speaking teachers of Japanese. Teachers have said that access to contemporary vocabulary and expressions is difficult without frequent immersion in Japan.

Vocabulary is categorized to help the teacher access information. The organizing principles are language functions or topical categories. Levels are not specified, as the teacher's materials and priorities will play a part in selecting vocabulary for a given course. By not assigning vocabulary to each developmental level, the message should be clear that vocabulary needs to be constantly reinforced. Words learned early on in one's study of a language are still going to be used later.

Resources

One of the components of this guide is a section of resources. The purpose is to help the teacher, especially the non-native teacher, by providing vocabulary and expressions that are not easily obtained and can only be learned through immersion in Japan. These are not required elements of a curriculum, but are support for the teacher.

List of Functions and Expressions

The generic listing of language functions (Scarino, et al., 1988) and related expressions in Japanese has been created to focus on what students might say to accomplish a given language purpose. The idea is not to move from a language function to the grammatical structure used in expressing that function; rather, grammatical structures should be taught within functional language use. The function of requesting requires certain structures, for example, *te* form of the verb + *kudasai;* however, a lot more verbal and nonverbal expression is needed to fulfill the language function. So, in this curriculum, a composite list of functions and corresponding expressions is provided. Generally, the expressions are given in formal style. But less formal equivalents are provided as necessary and appropriate.

General Vocabulary

A list of general vocabulary is also provided in the resources section. This is vocabulary that has been pulled from the various themes, vocabulary that is repeated and used in more than one theme. This listing supports the more thematically related vocabulary found at the end of each theme.

References

American Council on the Teaching of Foreign Language. *Proficiency Guidelines*. Yonkers, NY: ACTFL, 1986.

Brown, James Dean. *The Elements of Language Curriculum*. Boston, MA: Heinle and Heinle, 1995.

National Association of District Supervisors of Foreign Language. "Characteristics of Effective Foreign Language Instruction Guidelines." Unpublished Document, 1991.

National Foreign Language Center. A *Framework for Introductory Japanese Language Curricula in American High Schools and Colleges*. Washington, DC: National Foreign Language Center, 1993.

National Standards in Foreign Language Education Project. *Standards for Foreign Language Learning: Preparing for the 21st Century*. (Forthcoming in 1996.)

Omaggio Hadley, Alice. *Teaching Language in Context*. Boston, MA: Heinle and Heinle, 1993.

Scarino, Angela, et al. *Australian Language Levels Guidelines*. Canberra, Australia: Curriculum Development Centre, 1988.

Themes 2

Overview of Format

Themes

The twelve themes of this guide are content areas for focusing student learning and use of Japanese.

Levels

Each theme spreads across two to four language levels: beginning, transitional, intermediate, and advanced.

Outcomes	Suggested Assessment Activities
Outcomes describe what the student will be able to do with the language. From level to level, the student is challenged to achieve increasing proficiency in using Japanese. Selection of outcomes has been made on the basis of real and motivating applications for language use.	These activities describe how the student may demonstrate successful achievement of the outcomes. They are equally appropriate as learning activities or as opportunities for assessing student progress. Outcomes may be demonstrated in more than one skill area (listening, speaking, reading, and writing).

Language Components

Context
This provides critical questions as areas for exploration. Through the context, the student has a purpose for learning and using Japanese. Cultural topics are not specified, rather content is suggested that will match both the student's linguistic ability and cognitive development.

Sample Expressions	Structure
These statements, questions, or rejoinders represent natural language that would be used to achieve the purpose described in each outcome. The expressions further clarify what students should be able to do with the language. The *masu* and *desu* forms are used.	Drawn from the sample expressions, these are generalized structures to show teachers how knowledge of structures moves across levels from awareness, to a manipulative ability, to a secure usage of a given structure. Structures are reintroduced across levels. The dictionary form of verbs is used.

In the representation of structures and expressions, the following symbols are used:
... = sentences
~ = words or phrases
# = a number
A:/B: = an exchange between two people

Vocabulary

This listing suggests some of the breadth and depth of content appropriate to each level of a theme. Vocabulary derives from the context and sample expressions, and gives examples of what students might use to demonstrate achievement of each outcome.

 *Daily Routines*

Beginning Level

Outcomes	Suggested Assessment Activities
1. Student describes (orally and in writing) daily routines of self and others.	A. Student interviews classmates to find out their daily routine and summarizes the findings of the survey on a chart. B. Using pictures of daily routines on separate cards, student interviews a partner and puts the pictures in chronological order according to the partner's daily routines.
2. Student describes how often others perform various daily routine activities.	A. After interviewing another person, student reports on the frequency and time at which that person performs various routines (such as always exercises, sometimes eats breakfast, and so forth).

Beginning Level

Language Components

Context
Meal ● What is typically eaten at each meal? ● Who is typically present to eat a given meal? ● Who prepares each meal? ● Where are meals typically eaten? **School** ● What subjects do students study? ● In what after-school activities do students participate? ● What is the school calendar? **Bathing** ● How frequently and for how long does one typically bathe? ● What is the customary process? **Leisure/Free time activities** ● What are typical routine leisure activities? ● When, where, and with whom are they engaged in?

Sample Expressions	Structure
何時に起きますか。	なんじに
私は毎日六時半に起きます。	time に
七時に朝ごはんを食べます。	～を V
学校は朝八時から午後三時までです。	time から time まで
一時間目は数学です。	#じかんめ
八時から学校で勉強します。	time から/ place で
四時半までテニスをします。	sports をする
五時にうちへ帰ります。	place へ
テレビを見ます。それから、音楽を聞きます。	それから、
お風呂に入りますか。朝シャワーを浴びますか。	…か。…か。
晩ごはんはいつもお母さんと食べます。	someone と
よく、映画を見ますか。	よく
A:私は一日に四回、歯をみがきます。 B:うわぁ、すごいですね。	period of time に#かい
A:私はいつも五時に起きます。 B:へえ、早いですねえ。私は七時に起きます。	…ねえ

Transitional Level

Outcomes	Suggested Assessment Activities
1. Student explains how his or her routine is similar and different to another's.	A. Student listens to recorded interviews or reads about Japanese teenagers' daily routines and records key details of each person's routine on a grid. Student then provides information about his or her own routine and provides a comparison.
2. Student makes alternative plans when his or her daily routine causes a conflict or is interrupted.	A. Using the phone, student suggests and agrees on a new activity when partner tells of a conflict with a regularly planned activity.

Language Components

Context
Personal experiences ● What changes occur depending on one's situation or age? ● What behaviors or practices are prohibited or allowed at home, at school, and in society at large? **Daily routines of a teenager** ● What do teenagers do in school? ● What do teenagers do outside of school? ● What clothing is appropriate and customary? **Differences in daily routines** ● What differences are caused by age? ● What differences are caused by occupations? ● What differences are rooted in culture? ● What differences are due to changes in society?

Sample Expressions	Structure
七時半にうちを出ます。	place をでる
七時四十五分に学校に着きます。	place につく
放課後は毎日部活があります。	Nがある
部活は剣道部に入っています。	organization にはいっている
私は土曜日も日曜日も忙しいです。	～も～も
毎日学校の宿題が多くて大変です。	Adj (i) stem くて
食べる前に手を洗います。	～まえに
私は宿題をしてからテレビを見ます。	～てから
A:映画に行きましょう。 B:今日はピアノのレッスンがあるからだめです。	～ましょう …から…
水曜日なら大丈夫です。	～なら
木曜のほうがいいです。	～のほうがいい
それよりプールにしましょうか。	～にする

Vocabulary

Time

あさ	朝	morning
ひる	昼	noon
よる	夜	night
ばん	晩	evening
ひるま	昼間	daytime
いま	今	now
まえ	前	before
むかし	昔	a long time ago
しょうらい	将来	in the future
みらい	未来	future

Meals

しょくじ	食事	meals
ごはん	御飯	meals/cooked rice
あさごはん	朝御飯	breakfast
ひるごはん	昼御飯	lunch
ばんごはん	晩御飯	dinner/supper
ちょうしょく	朝食	breakfast
ちゅうしょく	昼食	lunch
ゆうしょく	夕食	supper
やしょく	夜食	late-night snack
おやつ		snack
おちゃ	お茶	tea
～はい	～杯	counting unit by container
おかわり		second helping
したく	支度	preparation
あとかたずけ	後片付け	clean up
おさら	お皿	plate/dish
ちゃわん		rice bowl

Bathing

シャワー		shower
ふろ	風呂	bath
タオル		towel
せっけん	石鹸	soap
シャンプー		shampoo
リンス		rinse

Words Related to After-school Activities

おけいこごと／レッスン	お稽古ごと	lessons taken after school (nonacademic)
じゅく	塾	cram school
アルバイト		part-time job

Bedding

ふとん	布団	*futon* (bedding)
ベッド		bed
シーツ		sheets
もうふ	毛布	blanket
まくら	枕	pillow

Descriptors

きれい（な）		pretty/clean
べんり（な）	便利（な）	convenient
ふべん（な）	不便（な）	inconvenient
おなじ	同じ	same

Verbs

あらう	洗う	to wash
あびる	浴びる	to bathe
みがく	磨く	to polish/brush
きがえる	着替える	to change
つくる	作る	to make
しく（ふとん）	敷く（布団）	to spread
はたらく	働く	to work
くつろぐ		to relax
あそぶ	遊ぶ	to play at leisure
やすむ	休む	to rest

Miscellaneous

にちじょうせいかつ	日常生活	daily life
にっき	日記	diary

Home and Community

Beginning Level

Outcomes	Suggested Assessment Activities
1. Student demonstrates knowledge of greeting and leave-taking practices.	A. Student identifies the hierarchical relationship between speakers in a conversation involving greeting or leave-taking. B. Given a time of day and/or situation, students greet each other appropriately.
2. Student describes an environment familiar to him or her.	A. Student describes any special characteristics about his or her home or school. B. Student answers questions on a survey related to the basic characteristics of his or her community.
3. Student expresses familiarity with the environment, and plant and animal life.	A. Given a verbal description of an animal, student identifies the animal. B. Student describes the name, color, and habitat of a plant or animal.

Language Components

Context
Greeting and leave-taking • What differences exist for talking to family members, friends, teachers, and adult acquaintances? **Neighborhoods** • What housing exists in a neighborhood? • What stores and public facilities exist in a neighborhood? • What occupations are found in a neighborhood? **Animals and their habitats** • What are the characteristics of different animals? • What do they eat? • Where do they live? • What animals are indigenous? • What animals are popular as pets?

Sample Expressions	Structure
A: いってきます。 B: いってらっしゃい。車に気をつけてね。	
A: 先生、さようなら。 B: 皆さん、さようなら。	
失礼します。	
A: じゃあね。 B: また、あした。	
A: ただいま。 B: お帰りなさい。	
いただきます。	
ごちそうさまでした。	
お休みなさい。	
私のうちは小さいうちです。	Adj + N
窓が五つあります。	〜が # ある
うちはマンションの5階です。	NのN
A: 近所に何がありますか。 B: 花屋とか本屋とか病院などがあります。	place に〜がある 〜とか〜とか〜など
A: どんな所ですか。 B: 森や湖に近くて静かなところです。	Adj (i) stem くて、Adj (na) + N
カラスは黒くてカーカーと鳴きます。	onomatopoeia と
花水木の花は白かピンクです。	〜か〜

Transitional Level

Outcomes	Suggested Assessment Activities
1. Student relays or follows directions to a location.	A. Student writes directions from school to his or her home, including important landmarks and descriptors. B. Student follows directions to locate a desired destination.
2. Student describes his or her home and community.	A. Showing a picture or drawing of his or her room or residence, student describes its contents and surroundings.
3. Student exhibits culturally appropriate behaviors and expressions when visiting Japanese homes.	A. Students perform in-class simulations of customs practiced in Japanese homes. B. After watching a demonstration of various home activities, student contributes observations and completes a multiple choice assessment on knowledge of appropriate behaviors.

Language Components

Context
Cities or communities • What systems of transportation exist? • Who uses them? • What commercial, residential, industrial, and recreational facilities exist? Housing • What differences in housing can be attributed to culture? Etiquette in the home and community • What are the socially expected behaviors? • What are the culturally determined practices? • How have these practices changed over time?

Sample Expressions	Structure
駅から学校まで歩いて五分です。	place から place まで
この道をまっすぐ行くと、左側に交番があります。	…と
一階には洗面所や風呂場があって、二階には寝室が二つあります。	〜て 〜が#ある
日本のうちに上がる時は、玄関で靴を脱いでスリッパをはきます。	…とき
ベッドの下に日記があります。	〜のしたに〜がある
ソファの上にネコがいます。	〜のうえに〜がいる
ごめんください。	
おじゃまします。	
どうぞ、お上がりください。	
つまらないものですが、どうぞ。	
どうぞごゆっくり。	
おじゃましました。	
じゃ、これで失礼します。	
また、来てください。	

Intermediate Level

Outcomes	Suggested Assessment Activities
1. Student expresses familiarity with the environment and the cultural connotations associated with plant and animal life.	A. Student reads a folktale, either in Japanese or in student's own language, and then writes a folktale in Japanese depicting animals in their environment.
2. Student describes the region or nation in which he or she lives.	A. Student creates a brochure of a region or nation of his or her choice for Japanese visitors, including population, special events, character, and climate.
3. Student describes preferences concerning the environment in which he or she lives.	B. Student writes an essay on a favorite place, such as a room, a park, or a country, and relates what he or she likes to do there and why.

Language Components

Context
The environment • How are wild animals and their habitats treated? • How are animals depicted in literature and folktales? • What connotations for plants and animals exist in different cultures? Physical and human characteristics of a region or nation • What occupations exist in communities? • What creates a region's lifestyle? • What makes a community or region desirable or undesirable? • What makes a community or region unique or well known?

Sample Expressions	Structure
昔々ある所におじいさんとおばあさんがいました。	place に N がいる
近くの山に一匹のわるいタヌキが住んでいました。	#の〜
ウィスコンシン州は森林が多く、産業もさかんなところです。	Adj (i) stem く
人口は約500万人で、その54パーセントがドイツ系です。	…で、…
夏は釣りをしたり水上スキーをしたりします。	〜たり〜たりする
冬はスキーやスケートを楽しむことが出来ます。	〜や〜 〜ことができる
いま住んでいる所は緑が多いから好きです。	Relative clause + N …から
アメリカで一番好きなところはニューヨークです。	いちばん Adj + N
きれいな店がたくさんあって、にぎやかなので好きです。	…ので

Advanced Level

Outcomes	Suggested Assessment Activities
1. Student reports on family or community history.	A. Student writes an historical or biographical report based on information gathered through an interview with a member of his or her family or community.
2. Student draws hypotheses and predicts outcomes related to an issue.	A. Student studies an issue selected by the class and presents, in written Japanese, a prediction of the direction that issue will take and what role an individual can play in the issue.
3. Student uses Japanese to support opinions.	A. Students work in groups to create a dream home and then organize and present an ad campaign to sell it to a potential Japanese buyer. B. Students work in small groups on an assigned environmental or community issue and take a pro or con position to research. They then discuss their position with members of a group taking the opposing view.

Language Components

Context
Homes and communities • What gives a person a sense of being a member of a family and of a community? • What knowledge of the past does one learn through family and community? • How does a community change over time? **Community concerns** • What issues are important today locally, regionally, and internationally? • How and why does the focus of an issue change? • What factors affect one's attitude on an issue?

Sample Expressions	Structure
祖父は1920年から1950年にかけてミルウォーキーに住んでいました。	time から time にかけて
母方はドイツ系で、父方はイギリス系です。	country けい
そのころ、ここは小さな村でした。	〜のころ
村には、店が一軒しかなかったそうです。	〜しかない …そうだ
地球の環境をまもるために、私たち高校生はどんなことが出来るでしょうか。	〜ために
一人一人が省エネに気をつけることが必要です。	…こと
資源を再利用しないと資源不足になります。	…ないと
資源を大切にしなければなりません。	〜なければならない
車を運転するより、なるべく歩くようにしましょう。	〜より〜ようにする
この家にはプールとテラスがついています。	〜には
もっと原子力を利用したらいいと思います。	…とおもう
その意見に賛成です。	
太陽エネルギーの方がいいと思います。	〜のほうが Adj

Vocabulary

Parts of the House

いえ	家	house
へや	部屋	room
ろうか	廊下	hallway
やね	屋根	roof
てんじょう	天井	ceiling
かべ	壁	wall
ドア		door
まど	窓	window
ゆか	床	floor
かいだん	階段	stairs
にかい	二階	upstairs
ちかしつ	地下室	basement
やねうら	屋根裏	attic
げんかん	玄関	entrance
いま／リビングルーム	居間	living (family) room
だいどころ/キッチン	台所	kitchen
しょくどう／ダイニング	食堂	dining room
おてあらい／トイレ	お手洗い	toilet
せんめんじょ	洗面所	place to wash face
ふろば	風呂場	place to bathe
しんしつ	寝室	bedroom
こどもべや	子供部屋	children's room
ようま	洋間	Western-style room
わしつ	和室	Japanese-style room
おしいれ	押入	closet
とこのま	床の間	*tokonoma* (alcove)
ふすま		Japanese sliding door
しょうじ		sliding paper door
たたみ	畳	*tatami* (floor mat)

Exterior

れんがだて	煉瓦建	brick
いっこだて	一戸建	single family dwelling house
アパート		apartment
マンション		condominium
にわ	庭	garden
もん	門	fence/gate
しゃこ/ガレージ	車庫	garage
バルコニー／ベランダ		balcony/veranda
テラス		terrace

Furnishings

たんす		chest of drawers
きょうだい／ドレッサー	鏡台	dresser
ベッド		bed
ほんだな	本棚	bookshelf
ソファ		sofa
テーブル		table
いす	椅子	chair
つくえ	机	desk

ざぶとん	座布団	*zabuton* (floor cushion)
こたつ		table with heating system
ストーブ		heater
エアコン		air conditioner
テレビ		television
ビデオデッキ		VCR
ステレオ		stereo
カーテン		curtain
え	絵	picture
でんきスタンド	電気スタンド	lamp
でんしレンジ	電子レンジ	microwave oven
さらあらいき	皿洗い機	dishwasher
レンジ		stove
ながし	流し	sink
れいぞうこ	冷蔵庫	refrigerator
しょっきだな	食器棚	cupboard
せんたくき	洗濯機	washing machine
かんそうき	乾燥機	dryer

People and Places in One's Neighborhood

きんじょ	近所	neighborhood
みせ	店	shop
みせのひと／てんいん	店の人／店員	shopkeeper/salesperson
ほんや	本屋	bookstore
やっきょく	薬局	pharmacy
くすりや	薬屋	drugstore
おかしや	お菓子屋	confectionery store
くだものや	果物屋	fruit shop
じてんしゃや	自転車屋	bicycle shop
カメラや	カメラ屋	camera shop
はなや	花屋	florist
にくや	肉屋	butcher
さかなや	魚屋	fish store
パンや	パン屋	bakery
きっさてん	喫茶店	coffee shop
レストラン		restaurant
こうばん	交番	police box
けいさつ	警察	police
ゆうびんきょく	郵便局	post office
ぎんこう	銀行	bank
しょうぼうしょ	消防署	fire department
おうだんほどう	横断歩道	crosswalk
ちゅうしゃじょう	駐車場	parking ramp
デパート		department store
スーパー		supermarket
こうそうビル	高層ビル	high-rise building
しょうてんがい	商店街	shopping mall
モール		mall
ちかがい	地下街	underground shopping mall
こうじょう	工場	factory
ジム		gym
スポーツクラブ		sport club
ゴルフじょう	ゴルフ場	golf course

Natural Environment

しぜんかんきょう	自然環境	natural environment
やま	山	mountain
うみ	海	ocean
りく	陸	land
かわ	川	river
みずうみ	湖	lake
ぬま	沼	marsh/bog
そら	空	sky
もり／しんりん	森／森林	forest
みつりん	密林	jungle

Animals

やせいどうぶつ	野性動物	wild animal
とり	鳥	bird
かちく	家畜	domestic animal
ウシ	牛	cow/cattle
ウマ	馬	horse
ヒツジ	羊	sheep
ブタ	豚	pig
ニワトリ	鶏	chicken
クジラ	鯨	whale
オオカミ	狼	wolf
クマ	熊	bear
タヌキ	狸	*tanuki* (raccoon-like animal native to Japan)
アナグマ	穴熊	badger
アライグマ		raccoon
スカンク		skunk
リス		squirrel
ウサギ	兎	rabbit
コマドリ		robin

Plants

サクラ	桜	cherry
タケ	竹	bamboo
マツ	松	pine
タンポポ		dandelion
カシ	樫	oak
カエデ	楓	maple
シラカバ	白樺	birch

Family-related Terms

かくかぞく	核家族	core family
さんせだいかぞく	三世代家族	three-generation family
ちちかた	父方	father's side
ははかた	母方	mother's side
～けい	～系	of~descent

Environment-related Terms

いしき	意識	consciousness
かんきょうもんだい	環境問題	environmental problem
さんせいう	酸性雨	acid rain
オゾンそう	オゾン層	ozone layer
ねったいうりん	熱帯雨林	tropical rain forest

しがいせん	紫外線	ultraviolet ray
しげん	資源	resources
さいかつよう	再活用	recycle
ふようひん	不用品	items not needed anymore
ちゅうこひん	中古品	used items
さいりよう	再利用	reutilization
リサイクル		recycle
しょうエネ	省エネ	energy conservation
エネルギー		energy
りよう	利用	utilization
ふそく	不足	shortage
ちきゅう	地球	earth
ほご	保護	protect
ほごセンター	保護センター	sanctuary
せいそくち／すみか	生息地	habitat
こうがい	公害	pollution
たいきおせん	大気汚染	air pollution
へんか	変化	change

Descriptors

しずか（な）	静か（な）	quiet
にぎやか（な）		busy/loud
うつくしい	美しい	beautiful
きたない	汚い	dirty
きれい（な）		clean
ひあたりがよい	日当りが良い	sunny
ひあたりがわるい	日当りが悪い	not sunny
あんぜん（な）	安全（な）	safe
めいわく（な）	迷惑（な）	troublesome/annoying

Verbs

すむ	住む	to live
あがる（うち）	上がる	to get in the house
おじゃまする	お邪魔する	to interrupt
しつれいする	失礼する	to excuse oneself
まもる	守る	to protect
つく	付く	to be attached
りようする	利用する	to utilize
なく	鳴く	to cry (animal sound)
ぜつめつする	絶滅する	to become extinct
こわす	壊す	to break/destroy
なくなる		to be lost
あつめる	集める	to collect
へる	減る	to decrease
ふえる	増える	to increase
たりる	足りる	to be sufficient
ふそくする	不足する	to be short of
すすむ	進む	to progress
かいぜん（する）	改善（する）	to improve

Miscellaneous

むかしばなし	昔話	story from the past
みんわ	民話	folktale

 *Japan and the World*

Beginning Level

Outcomes	Suggested Assessment Activities
1. Student applies rules of Japanese pronunciation to Japanese words commonly used in English, such as karaoke, sake, ramen, kimono, and futon.	A. Student pronounces the sounds of the Japanese language accurately and identifies the romanized representation of those sounds.
2. Student deduces meaning of many words borrowed from English and written in katakana.	A. Student selects correct object when given a verbal cue. B. Seeing the word written in katakana for an object, student draws the object.
3. Student describes the degree of cross-cultural influences, such as music, commercial images, diet, fashion, and language, on a society.	A. Throughout the year, student watches the press and media for reports on Japan and brings articles to share and summarize in class. B. Student identifies words borrowed from the English language in contemporary Japanese music or magazines.
4. Student identifies and challenges stereotypes while developing cross-cultural understanding and exploring universal human values.	A. At the start of the year, student creates a poster depicting his or her own images of Japan. At the end of the year, student lists differences of his or her current view of Japan compared to his or her view at the beginning of the year.

Beginning Level

Language Components

Context
Culture ● How are elements of one culture borrowed by another culture? ● How do things change as they move from one culture to another? **Stereotypes** ● What creates stereotypes? ● What changes stereotypes?

Sample Expressions	Structure
言ってみましょう。	〜てみる
みんなで言ってください。	〜てください
いっしょに言ってください。	
ひとりずつ言ってみましょう。	#ずつ
もう一度言ってください。	
この言葉の意味は何ですか。	この〜
「チョコレート」はどれですか。	どれ
「ラジカセ」の絵をかいてください。	
「トレパン」のもとの言葉は何ですか。	

Transitional Level

Outcomes	Suggested Assessment Activities
1. Student demonstrates knowledge of the names of countries, languages, and peoples around the world.	A. Student completes a chart with missing information on the nationalities, languages spoken, and city of residence of several people from around the world and within Japan. The instructor serves as the provider of information, responding to oral questions posed by the students. Answers may be recorded in English. B. Student records the names of nations, languages, and peoples on a world map. C. Student writes the name of an individual on a map, indicating where that person is from in response to teacher cues.
2. Student describes the degree of global interdependence of nations for food and other resources.	A. Student answers questions based on a map of the world containing import-export data.
3. Student shows awareness of the dynamics of Japanese culture and draws comparisons between the Japan of the past and today's Japan.	A. Student identifies sentences as true of the Japan of yesterday or the Japan of today.

Transitional Level

Language Components

Context
Geography • How are political boundaries different from cultural and economic boundaries? • How has a language come to be spoken in a particular area? Cultural Change • How similar or different is past culture from present culture?

Sample Expressions	Structure
メキシコ人はスペイン語を話します。	～ご
ブラジルでは何語を話しますか。	placeでは
この国の名前は何ですか。	NのN
ここには、どんな人が住んでいますか。	～ている
お国はどちらですか。	どちら
スミスさんはアメリカの方です。	～のかた
ミケレスさんはギリシャ出身です。	～しゅっしん
オリーブ油はイタリーの特産品です。	
日本はフランスからワインを輸入しています。	place から
日本は自動車の輸出国です。	
日本人は昔は着物を着ていましたが、今は大抵洋服を着ています。	…が

Intermediate Level

Outcomes	Suggested Assessment Activities
1. Student draws conclusions from statistical information on a given global social issue.	A. Using charts, maps, and reference materials in Japanese, student works with a partner to locate the information needed to complete research requested on a task card (for example, compare five countries on population density).
2. Student predicts or describes the future.	A. Student writes an essay entitled, "In the Year 2010."

Intermediate Level

Language Components

Context
Global Comparisons • How does one make valid comparisons between cultures? • How similar or different is present culture from predictable future culture?

Sample Expressions	Structure
この表から何がわかりますか。	〜から
人口の一番多い国はどこですか。	いちばん Adj
一人あたりの牛肉の消費量はどのくらいですか。	
21世紀の世界はどんな世界だと思いますか。	…とおもう

Advanced Level

Outcomes	Suggested Assessment Activities
1. Student reports and draws conclusions from statistical information on a given global social issue.	A. Student makes a presentation using charts and other visual aids to illustrate the issue and support conclusions drawn.
2. Student reads and summarizes articles in Japanese on cross-cultural conflict or societal concerns within Japan.	A. Student summarizes main points from an article to the class and facilitates questions and comments.
3. Student demonstrates knowledge of international interdependence and shared global responsibility.	A. Student discusses daily news from an article he or she brought to class or accessed from a computerized news source.
4. Student applies problem-solving skills to facilitate conflict resolution.	A. Student participates in a role-play of a meeting of parties involved in a contemporary conflict and strives to negotiate a settlement or resolution. A conflict involving Japan and another nation would be most appropriate, but others may be considered. B. Student explains his or her interpretation of why a certain misunderstanding occurred, what cultural expectations were present, and how what transpired varied from those expectations. Student can draw from a personal experience or respond to a situation presented in class.
5. Student exhibits knowledge of key political, historical, and cultural figures in Japan's past and present.	A. Student researches and role-plays the personality to the class, responding to students' questions and relaying important information so students can complete a summary form.
6. Student shows understanding of the dynamics of Japanese culture and draws comparisons between the Japan of the past and today's Japan.	A. After hearing dialogues, student identifies them as being from contemporary Japan or from the Japan of yesterday.

Advanced Level

Language Components

Context
Culture • How has a culture been influenced by certain events and people? • What current issues are shaping the culture?

Sample Expressions	Structure
統計によると、この国の国民一人あたりの総生産数は世界一だそうです。	〜によると …そうだ
このグラフから大気汚染が進んでいることがわかります。	…こと
もしオゾン層の破壊がこれ以上進むと世界中で皮膚ガンが増えるでしょう。	もし…と
環境破壊を予防するためには、何をするべきだと思いますか。	〜べき
国と国との間の誤解を防ぐためには、個人間の相互理解が大切です。	〜ためには
一番大切なことはお互いの国の言葉を学ぶことではないでしょうか。	〜ではないでしょうか
私は「おいで、おいで」をしたつもりなのに、皆向こうに行ってしまいました。	〜たつもり…のに 〜てしまう
「中浜万次郎」のことを知っていますか。	〜のこと
「曙」になったつもりで話してください。	〜になったつもり

Vocabulary

Japanese Words Used in the U.S.

カラオケ		*karaoke*
さけ	酒	*sake*
すし	寿司	*sushi*
きもの	着物	*kimono*
おりがみ	折り紙	*origami*
とうふ	豆腐	*tofu*
ふとん	布団	*futon*
すきやき	すき焼き	*sukiyaki*
てりやき	照焼	*teriyaki*

U.S. Words Used in Japan

パソコン	personal computer
ラジカセ	tape deck
エアコン	air conditioning
トレパン	sweat pants
ハンバーガー	hamburger
ホットドック	hot dog
ピザ	pizza
コーヒー	coffee
コーラ	coke
オレンジジュース	orange juice
サウンド	sound
デビュー・アルバム	debut album
ポップス	popular music
ブーム	trend
コンビネーション	combination
コーディネーション	coordination
アイテム	item

Nationality/Language

メキシコ		Mexico
メキシコじん	メキシコ人	Mexican citizen
スペインご	スペイン語	Spanish language
ブラジル		Brazil
ブラジルじん		Brazilian citizen
ポルトガルご	ポルトガル語	Portuguese language
にほん	日本	Japan
にほんじん	日本人	Japanese citizen
にほんご	日本語	Japanese language
ちゅうごく	中国	China
ちゅうごくじん	中国人	Chinese citizen
ちゅうごくご	中国語	Chinese language
かんこく	韓国	Korea
かんこくじん	韓国人	Korean citizen
かんこくご／ハングル	韓国語／ハングル	Korean language

タイ		Thailand
タイじん	タイ人	Thai citizen
タイご	タイ語	Thai language
アメリカがっしゅうこく	アメリカ合衆国	The United States of America
アメリカじん	アメリカ人	U.S. citizen
イギリス		Great Britain/United Kingdom
イギリスじん	イギリス人	British citizen
オーストラリア		Australia
オーストラリアじん	オーストラリア人	Australian citizen
えいご	英語	English language
カナダ		Canada
カナダじん	カナダ人	Canadian citizen
えいご／フランスご	英語／フランス語	English/French language
ドイツ		Germany
ドイツじん	ドイツ人	German citizen
ドイツご	ドイツ語	German language
フランス		France
フランスじん	フランス人	French citizen
フランスご	フランス語	French language
イスラエル		Israel
イスラエルじん	イスラエル人	Israeli citizen
ヘブライご	ヘブライ語	Hebrew language
エジプト		Egypt
エジプトじん	エジプト人	Egyptian citizen
アラビアご	アラビア語	Arabic language

Trade/Economy

ぼうえき	貿易	trade
ぼうえきまさつ	貿易摩擦	trade friction
ゆにゅう（する）	輸入（する）	import
ゆしゅつ（する）	輸出（する）	export
ゆにゅう／ゆしゅつあいてこく	輸入／輸出相手国	trading partner
あかじ（になる）	赤字（になる）	deficit
くろじ（になる）	黒字（になる）	surplus
せきゆ	石油	oil
せきゆきき	石油危機	oil crisis
しょくりょう	食料	food
げんざいりょう	原材料	raw materials
かこうひん	加工品	processed food
じどうしゃ	自動車	automobile
ぶひん	部品	parts
でんきせいひん	電気製品	electric appliance
にほんせい（の）	日本製	made in Japan
がいこくせい（の）	外国製	foreign made
じきゅうりつ	自給率	rate of self-sufficiency
へんか	変化	change
ぞうか	増加	growth
ていか	低下	decline

Political Terms

こくみん	国民	people
こくみんせい	国民性	national characteristics
こくみんせいかつ	国民生活	people's lifestyle
こくみんしょとく	国民所得	income
こくみんそうせいさん	国民総生産	gross national product (GNP)
ぐんじりょく	軍事力	military power
～あたり		per
しゅようこく	主要国	major countries
せんしんしょこく	先進諸国	industrialized nations
はってんとじょうこく	発展途上国	developing nations
だい#い	第#位	the # (ordinals)
けいこう	傾向	tendency
ひかく	比較	comparison
せいちょう	成長	growth
しゃかいほしょう	社会保証	social security
ふくし	福祉	social welfare
ぜいきん	税金	tax
ふたん	負担	burden
ざいせい	財政	finance
りっこうほ	立候補	running for a position
せんきょ	選挙	election

Life Span Related

じんこう	人口	population
じんこうぞうか	人口増加	population growth
こうれいかしゃかい	高齢化社会	aging society
へいきんじゅみょう	平均寿命	average life span
だんせい	男性	male person
じょせい	女性	female person
いりょうひ	医療費	medical cost
もんだい	問題	problem
かだい	課題	issue
しょうらい	将来	future
せんご	戦後	after World War II
きんねん	近年	recently
きゅうそくに	急速に	rapidly
しゃかいげんしょう	社会現象	social phenomenon

Geographic Terms

ちず	地図	map
せかい	世界	world
きたはんきゅう	北半球	Northern Hemisphere
みなみはんきゅう	南半球	Southern Hemisphere
たいりく	大陸	continent
しま	島	island
はんとう	半島	peninsula
ぐんとう	群島	archipelago
しょとう	諸島	islands
わん	湾	bay/gulf
わんがん	湾岸	shoreline
さばく	砂漠	desert
へいや	平野	plain/open field
ぼんち	盆地	valley

さんち	山地	mountainous district
さんみゃく	山脈	mountain range
かざん	火山	volcano
たいへいよう	太平洋	Pacific Ocean
たいせいよう	大西洋	Atlantic Ocean
インドよう	インド洋	Indian Ocean
ほっかい	北海	North Sea
ひょうざん	氷山	iceberg
ひょうが	氷河	glacier

History-related Terms

#せいき	#世紀	century
～じだい	～時代	era/period
ならじだい	奈良時代	Nara period
へいあんじだい	平安時代	Heian period
かまくらじだい	鎌倉時代	Kamakura period
えどじだい	江戸時代	Edo period
めいじじだい	明治時代	Meiji period
いせき	遺跡	ruins

Political/Historical/Cultural Figures

しょうとくたいし	聖徳太子	Prince Shotoku
むらさきしきぶ	紫式部	Lady Murasaki
みなもとよりとも	源頼朝	Shogun Yoritomo
フランシスコ・ザビエル		Francisco Xavier
とくがわいえやす	徳川家康	The first Tokugawa Shogunate
まつおばしょう	松尾芭蕉	Basho
かくしかほくさい	葛飾北斎	Hokusai
なかはままんじろう	中浜万次郎	Manjiro Nakahama
めいじてんのう	明治天皇	Emperor Meiji
しょうわてんのう	昭和天皇	Emperor Showa
あけぼの	曙	Akebono

Natural Resources/Agricultural Products

しょくりょう	食料	food
トウモロコシ		corn
ココア		cocoa
らくのうせいひん	酪農製品	dairy products
しょくにく	食肉	meat
すいさんぶつ	水産物	products from the sea
てっこうせき	鉄鉱石	mineral resources
ウラン		uranium
ダイアモンド		diamond
せきゆ	石油	oil
せきたん	石炭	coal

Verbs

たよる	頼る	to rely on
はってんする	発展する	to develop
こえる	超える	to surpass
すすむ	進む	to make progress
かいぜんする	改善する	to improve
のびる	伸びる	to grow

Leisure / Free Time

Beginning Level

Outcomes	Suggested Assessment Activities
1. Student expresses his or her preferences of leisure activities.	A. Given pictures of different leisure activities, student selects one and expresses whether he or she likes it or not. B. Student summarizes class survey, making comparisons about its results (for example, A likes skiing, but B does not, and C likes tennis the best).
2. Student describes personal use of leisure time.	A. Given information on a Japanese young person's leisure activities, student describes similarities and differences, including where, how often, and with whom the student performs the same activities.
3. Student demonstrates an activity, using phrases and gestures to bypass complicated vocabulary and structures.	A. Student explains an action (such as swimming or painting), using strategies and key descriptive words including "about this big," "lightly," "this way," "more or less," "quickly," "like this," or "not like that."
4. Student makes arrangements with a friend to engage in a leisure activity, refusing or accepting appropriately.	A. Student calls a friend on the phone and invites him or her to participate in an activity. The invitee either accepts or refuses. B. Student compares his or her schedule to a friend's schedule and negotiates when to meet for a given activity.
5. Student orders a meal from a menu.	A. Student role-plays either the wait staff or a customer, asking and answering questions with expressions commonly used in restaurants.
6. Student participates in a simple Japanese game.	A. Student plays a simple game using Japanese conventions for choosing teams, assigning team names, keeping score, cheering on team members, and so forth.
7. Student deduces key information from authentic documents.	A. Student skims and scans a poster advertising an event (such as a sports festival, movie, or club meeting) to determine the date, time, location, cost, and so forth.

Beginning Level

Language Components

Context
Activities of youth • What activities are universally enjoyed which are more culturally specific? • What are the procedures and customs for participating in various leisure activities? • How do people in a culture ask others to join in leisure activities, and how does one respond to such an invitation? Description of interests • What influence does culture have on how one's abilities are discussed?

Sample Expressions	Structure
私はテニスが好きです。	〜は〜がすき
ぼくはテニスは好きじゃないです。	〜は〜ない
朝子さんはテニスが好きですが、夕子さんはあまり好きではありません。	…が、 あまり…ない
太郎くんはテニスが一番好きです。	〜がいちばん
いつも学校のテニスコートでテニスをします。	N の N place で
週に二回友達とテニスをします。	period of time に #かい
ラケットはこう持ちます。	こう
こうやってボールを打ちます。	こうやって
ラケットは軽く降ってください。	Adj (i) stem く
そうやってはだめです。	〜てはだめ／〜ちゃだめ
明日テニスをしませんか。	〜ませんか
三時にテニスコートで会いましょう。	time に place で
明日はちょっと。	
いらっしゃいませ。こちらへどうぞ。	
ビザとスパゲティをお願いします。	〜と〜
じゃんけんでチームを決めましょう。	〜ましょう
勝った。負けた。	V た
がんばれ!	
映画会は3月3日の四時半からです。	time から
学生は500円です。	

Transitional Level

Outcomes	Suggested Assessment Activities
1. Student describes steps in a simple sequence.	A. Student explains in Japanese how to play a simple children's game from his or her own culture. B. Student puts together a recipe.
2. Student skims and scans written script or text to find out specific information.	A. Student skims and scans the sports page of a newspaper to find scores or results of recent games. B. Student skims and scans a newspaper or entertainment guide to determine the details of leisure activities. C. Student reads a chart or survey on how people spend their leisure time and summarizes the results in spoken or written form.
3. Student expresses preferences to various activities, describes the degree to which he or she can or cannot participate in various activities, and gives a reason for or against participation.	A. After student creates a list of excuses, he or she takes a card illustrating an activity and explains why he or she can or cannot participate in that activity by selecting an appropriate excuse. B. Student decides on a leisure activity and gives reasons for the choice. C. Student writes a short composition on how he or she spends his or her leisure time and why.
4. Student politely gives, accepts, and refuses invitations.	A. After picking a card describing a person, student writes a short note of invitation based on the person's status and age. B. After picking a card describing a person's status and age, student indicates acceptance or refusal of an invitation from that person.

Transitional Level

Language Components

Context
Use of leisure time • What expressions and customs are culturally appropriate for making arrangements for leisure activities? • How strongly do age, culture, family, and environment influence one's use of free time? • What sports are encouraged or practiced in a culture or region? • What types of entertainment are common in various age groups and various cultures?

Sample Expressions	Structure
はじめにじゃんけんで、おにを決めます。	はじめに
次に、おには目かくしをして「十」数えます。	つぎに
その間に、みんな隠れます。	そのあいだに
おには「十」数えた後で、みんなを探します。	〜たあとで
卵を入れる前に、砂糖を入れてください。	〜まえに
卵を入れてから、よく混ぜます。	〜てから
最後に、オーブンで焼きます。	さいごに
三対二でジャイアンツが勝ちました。	#たい#
その映画なら土曜日までやっています。	〜なら
新聞によると、連休には約10万人の人が海外へ出かけたそうです。	〜によると…そうだ
スケートはあまり得意じゃないから、したくありません。	…から
今日は足が痛いから、テニスはしません。	…から
今日は天気がいいから、テニスにしましょう。	〜にする
ひまだったら、来ませんか。	…たら
その日ならちょうど空いています。	〜なら
せっかくですが、その日はちょっと。	…が

Intermediate Level

Outcomes	Suggested Assessment Activities
1. Student explains a leisure activity.	A. Student gives an in-class demonstration of a personal hobby or activity. B. Student selects an object used for a leisure activity (such as a kendo stick or baseball bat) and spontaneously gives an oral explanation and demonstration.
2. Student interprets for an English speaker.	A. After listening to a live presentation about a favorite pastime, student asks questions for clarification and summarizes presentation for an English-speaking audience.
3. Student demonstrates awareness of popular personal and professional leisure activities in Japan.	A. After writing a survey to find out how students spend their free time, student conducts the survey with U.S. students and Japanese sister school students via letter, fax, or video, and then analyzes the similarities and differences.

Intermediate Level

Language Components

Context
Invitations   • How does the form of an invitation differ according to status, age, or gender?   • How does a person politely accept or refuse an invitation?   **Leisure activities**   • What leisure activities are enjoyed by Japanese people of various ages?   • How have popular leisure activities changed over time?   • How do leisure activities change when adopted by another culture?

Sample Expressions	Structure
このゲームのやり方について説明します。	〜について
まず、カードを五枚ずつ配ります。	#ずつ
ピッチャーがボールを投げたら、バットで打ちます。	…たら、 〜で (by means of)
ゴルフのクラブは、このように持ちます。	このように
ひじを伸ばしたまま、後ろに降り上げます。	〜たまま
そのまま、まっすぐ降ろします。	そのまま
毎日三時からプールで泳ぐんですね。	…ね。
費用はあまりかからないんですね。	かかる(cost)
水着だけ持っていけばいいんですね。	〜だけ、 …ば
すみません。もう一度おねがいします。	
好きなこと／得意なことは何ですか。	Adj (na) +こと
暇な時間があったら、どんなことをして過ごしますか。	…たら
何かアルバイトをしていますか。	なにか
週に何時間ぐらい働きますか。	period of time に#じかん

Advanced Level

Outcomes	Suggested Assessment Activities
1. Student describes a leisure activity in detail to a Japanese person who may not be familiar with it.	A. Student selects a picture of one of various kinds of leisure activities and describes in detail what is involved, including any cultural connotations. B. Using a chart, visual, or manipulative (such as a school yearbook) related to leisure activities, student explains the activity (such as school clubs) in a presentation or lecture format to communicate information.
2. Student writes a multi-paragraph composition on leisure activities.	A. Student writes a composition describing an ideal family vacation in the past or the future.

Language Components

Context
Leisure activities • What leisure activities are not common among the people of Japan? • How are Japanese and U.S. students' use of free time similar and different? • What influences one's choice of how to celebrate a holiday? • What influences one's choice of vacation plans?

Sample Expressions	Structure
このゲームは日本人にはとても珍しいのではないでしょうか。	…ではないでしょうか／だろうか。
日本では見られないと思います。	みる／みられる (potential) ない
これはこの地方に古くから伝わる伝統的な遊びです。	Relative clause + N
このゲームの遊び方を詳しく説明しますと次のようになります。	〜のようになる
これには大自然を体験するといういみがあります。	…というN
どんな休暇が理想的だと思いますか。	…とおもう
日本で一番人気のあるレジャーは、温泉に行くことだそうです。	…そうだ
何といっても家族旅行が一番だと思います。	N がいちばん
家族そろってキャンプに行きたいと思います。	
将来、家族で宇宙旅行するようになるかもしれませんね。	…ようになるかもしれない

Vocabulary

Games

おに		it (when playing a game)
めかくし	目かくし	blindfold
じゃんけん		*jan-ken* (paper, stone, scissors)
かくれんぼ		hide and seek
おにごっこ		tag
てつぼう	鉄棒	ironbar
ブランコ		swing
なわとび		jump rope
テレビゲーム		video game
トランプ		deck of cards
カルタ		*karuta* (Japanese card game)
カード		card

Hobbies

しゅみ	趣味	hobbies

Reading

どくしょ	読書	reading
しょうせつ	小説	novel
たんていしょうせつ	探偵小説	detective stories
どうわ	童話	fairy tale
ものがたり	物語	story
でんき	伝記	biography
まんが	漫画	comic book
ざっし	雑誌	magazine
しんぶん	新聞	newspaper

Music

おんがくかんしょう	音楽鑑賞	music appreciation
ロック		rock music
ポピュラー（ポップ）		popular songs
ジャズ		jazz
クラシック		classical music

Movie

えいが	映画	movie
スリラー		thriller
ドキュメンタリー		documentary
ノンフィクション		nonfiction
エスエフ		science fiction
ロマンス		romance
ミュージックビデオ		music video

Sports

スポーツ		sports
スケートボード		skateboard
ローラーブレード		roller-blade
スキー		skiing
スケート		skating
ダイビング		scuba diving

バスケットボール		basketball
テニス		tennis
フットボール		football
バレーボール		volleyball
すもう	相撲	sumo wrestling
けんどう	剣道	*kendo*
じゅうどう	柔道	*judo*
からて	空手	*karate*
プロレス		pro wrestling
やきゅう	野球	baseball
ハンティング		hunting
アメリカンフットボール		American football
チーム		team
チアリーダー		cheerleader
スノーモービル		snowmobile
モーターボート		motorboat

Leisure Activities

りょこう	旅行	traveling
おんせん	温泉	hot spring
やまのぼり（とざん）	山登り（登山）	mountain climbing
ミュージカル		musical
コンサート		concert
かぞくりょこう	家族旅行	traveling with family
オートキャンプ		auto camping
がいしょく	外食	eating out
カラオケ		*karaoke*

Places

こうえん	公園	park
えいがかん	映画館	movie theater
げきじょう	劇場	theater
～ホール		hall
レストラン		restaurant

Eating Out

メニュー		menu
すしや	寿司屋	*sushi* restaurant
そばや		*soba* restaurant
わしょく	和食	Japanese food
やきとり	焼鳥	*yakitori* (chicken kabob)
きっさてん	喫茶店	coffee shop
ハンバーガーショップ		hamburger shop
フランスりょうり	フランス料理	French food
ちゅうかりょうり	中華料理	Chinese food
エスニックりょうり	エスニック料理	ethnic food
タイりょうり	タイ料理	Thai food

Cooking

たまご	卵	egg
さとう	砂糖	sugar
しお	塩	salt
こしょう	故障	pepper
しょうゆ	醤油	*shoyu* (soy sauce)
みそ	味噌	*miso* (soybean paste)

す	酢	vinegar
こむぎこ	小麦粉	flour
ベーキングパウダー		baking powder
バター		butter
バニラ		vanilla
オーブン		oven

Lessons

クラス		class
レッスン		lesson
バレー		ballet
ダンス		dancing
ピアノ		piano
ギター		guitar
そろばん		abacus
がいこくご	外国語	foreign language
とうろく	登録	registration
ひよう	費用	cost
げっしゃ	月謝	monthly fee
かいひ	会費	meeting fee
かいいん/メンバー	会員	member
かいいんしょう	会員証	member's identification
ようい	用意	preparation
ふくそう	服装	clothing/attire
よてい	予定	schedule/plan
ばん	番	turn

Holidays

きゅうじつ	休日	holiday
きゅうか	休暇	vacation
れんきゅう	連休	long weekend
どにち	土日	Saturday and Sunday
しゅうまつ	週末	weekend

Descriptors

おもしろい	面白い	interesting
つまらない		boring
おかしい		funny
たのしい	楽しい	enjoyable
きれい（な）		pretty
ゆかい（な）	愉快（な）	fun
きけん（な）	危険（な）	danger

Verbs

でかける	出かける	to go out
あう	会う	to meet
さそう	誘う	to ask/invite
ことわる	断わる	to refuse
うける	受ける	to accept
すごす	過ごす	to spend time
まぜる	混ぜる	to mix
かぞえる	数える	to count
さがす	探す	to search/look for
いれる	入れる	to put in
くばる	配る	to distribute

なげる	投げる	to throw
うつ	打つ	to hit
ける	蹴る	to kick
かかる		to cost
たのしむ	楽しむ	to enjoy

Miscellaneous

アンケートちょうさ	アンケート調査	questionnaire
ひま	暇	free time
りそうてき	理想的	ideal

 *Means of Communication*

Beginning Level

Outcomes	Suggested Assessment Activities
1. Student inquires about availability and location of various means of communication.	A. Student reacts to a memo requesting a response by phone, fax, or letter by asking where to find the service and indicating where it exists. Teacher plays the role of information desk manager or concierge.
2. Student demonstrates understanding of the role of business cards in communication when interacting with Japanese persons.	A. Student performs self introduction with teacher and fellow students, applying appropriate stance, bows, card exchange etiquette, and expressions. B. Given a business card, student identifies key information.
3. Student demonstrates culturally appropriate active listening techniques using verbal and nonverbal feedback, showing awareness of the potential for cross-cultural misunderstanding that may evolve from misinterpreted nonverbal cues.	A. Student responds to a video or audio cassette with feedback such as head nodding, aizuchi, and so forth. B. Student records observations of such feedback while viewing an interaction. C. Student displays active listening techniques in response to a teacher-presented monologue.
4. Student leaves information for a return call on an answering machine.	A. Student hears answering machine message and leaves basic information needed in order to receive a return call.
5. Student writes brief functional notes in kana and kanji.	A. Student writes an invitation for a party he or she is giving. B. Student writes a thank-you note to a friend for a gift received. C. Student completes simple (simulated-authentic) personal data form (such as for a host family) describing personal interests, leisure activities, and so forth. D. Student writes a short note inviting a friend to participate together in some activity in the near future.

Beginning Level

Language Components

Context
Communicating globally and locally ● How does one use different technology for communication around the world (such as telephone and answering machine, fax, mail, and e-mail)? ● How does the availability and cost of communication compare around the world? ● What are the rituals and practices associated with business cards? **Active listening** ● How important is nonverbal and verbal feedback in communication? ● What cultural understanding is necessary for effective communication? **Written communication** ● What format is used for written communication in different cultures? ● When, to whom, and how are messages or memos written?

Sample Expressions	Structure
電話はどこにありますか。	〜は place にある
この店にファックスがありますか。	place に〜がある
郵便局はどこでしょうか。	どこ
電話をかけたいんですが。	〜たいんですが
これはぼくの名刺です。	N の N
これが電話番号です。	〜が
はい、はい。	
ええ。	
うん、うん、ふうん。	
ああ、そうですか。	
ほんとに!	
そうですねえ。	
へえ。	
うちの電話番号は623-2753です。	#の#
あとでお電話下さい。	あとで
私の誕生パーティーに来てください。	〜てください Adj (na) + N
すてきなプレゼントをありがとうございました。	
来週、映画に行きませんか。	…ませんか

Transitional Level

Outcomes	Suggested Assessment Activities
1. Student uses the phone to make arrangements or exchange information.	A. Student receives permission to not complete a homework assignment by calling the instructor and explaining why he or she cannot finish the assignment. B. With a partner, student writes and performs telephone conversations between two friends making arrangements to meet for a chosen activity.
2. Student exchanges information or ideas with others through a note or letter.	A. Student writes and exchanges letters with the instructor or fellow students on a given topic. B. Student writes and exchanges letters with members of another Japanese language class or with a sister-school class in Japan. Information learned through such letters can then be reported to others in class.
3. Student demonstrates understanding of messages left on an answering machine.	A. Student leaves a message asking questions or requesting specific information. Another student "calls back" and leaves a message with the information requested.
4. Student knows the meaning of visual signs and symbols in Japan.	A. Student directs others to a phone, subway, or post office by recognizing the symbol or sign used to depict such a location. B. Given a sign, student tells in Japanese what he or she may or may not do.

Language Components

Context
The telephone
● Does the process for making a phone call differ around the world?
● What cultural knowledge or etiquette should one know?
Letter writing
● What is the appropriate letter-writing format in a given culture?
● What elements are customary to include when writing letters?
● What cultural expectations exist regarding the content of a letter?
Signs
● What messages are important to understand from signs?
● What can one understand about culture through interpreting public signs?

Sample Expressions	Structure
もしもし、山田先生のお宅ですか。	
3年2組の田中ですが、山田先生はいらっしゃいますか。	いる／いらっしゃる
風邪のため宿題が出来ませんでした。	〜のため
レポートを明後日出してもいいですか。	〜てもいい
A:明日、映画に行きませんか。 B:明日は、ちょっと。	〜ませんか
A:何時にしましょうか。 B:三時はどうですか。	〜にする 〜はどう
毎日暑いですが、お元気ですか。	…が
では、お元気で。さようなら。	
ただ今、留守にしています。	
ビーという音のあとでメッセージをお残しください。	〜 のあとで お V ください
もしもし、夕子ですが、明日のパーティーは何時からでしたか。	〜でしたか
もしもし、朝子ですが、昨日うちにめがねを忘れませんでしたか。	〜ませんでしたか
あとでまた、こちらからお電話します。	
車は入ってはいけません。	〜てはいけない
芝生に入らないでください。	〜ないでください

Intermediate Level

Outcomes	Suggested Assessment Activities
1. Student enters and edits documents in Japanese on a computer.	A. Student enters an essay or paragraph from his or her textbook on the computer, edits it, and submits it to the instructor. B. Student sends and responds to e-mail messages from teachers or classmates. C. Student writes an article in Japanese for publication in a newsletter or newspaper.
2. Student receives and transmits information using computer or fax technology.	A. Students conduct surveys by fax or computer networking with students in another Japanese language class or a class in Japan.
3. Student interprets content of authentic handwritten text.	A. Student answers questions about the content of a letter handwritten by a native speaker of Japanese. B. Student reads a handwritten letter and, through context, attempts to define the meaning of unknown words. Finally, student checks hypotheses by using Japanese dictionaries.
4. Student communicates in a formal written style.	A. Student writes a formal letter.

Language Components

Context
Technology in communication • What changes in communication customs have occurred due to development and availability of advanced technology? • How has technology influenced the etiquette of communication? Handwritten script • When is it appropriate to communicate in handwritten form rather than typed print? • Are penmanship and calligraphy still considered to be a very important skill? Formal letter format • What changes are occurring in style and form?

Sample Expressions	Structure
No sample expressions and structures are given for this theme's intermediate level outcomes. In order to achieve the outcomes, the teacher will integrate the language components from other themes. Means of Communication is a theme to be taught over the course of an entire year.	

Vocabulary

Communication Method

でんわ	電話	telephone
ポケベル		pager
るすでん	留守電	answering machine
ファックス		fax (facsimile)
パソコン		personal computer
でんしメール	電子メール	e-mail
ぶんつう	文通	correspondence
てがみ	手紙	letter
ふうとう	封筒	envelope
きって	切手	stamps
そくたつ	速達	special delivery
かきとめ	書留	registered mail
はがき	葉書	postcard
えはがき	絵葉書	picture postcard
メモ		memo
ことづけ		message
メッセージ		message
ワープロ		word processor
てがき	手書き	handwritten
いんさつ	印刷	printed
おと	音	sound
おしらせ	お知らせ	announcement
けいじばん	掲示板	bulletin board
れんらく	連絡	contact
ニュースレター		newsletter
しんぶん	新聞	newspaper
きじ	記事	article

Socialization

ねんがじょう	年賀状	New Year's card
しょちゅうみまい	暑中みまい	summer greeting card
たんじょうカード	誕生カード	birthday card
あいさつじょう	挨拶状	letter of greeting
れいじょう	礼状	thank you card
めいし	名刺	calling/business card
めいしこうかん	名刺交換	exchange of greeting card
あいづち		aizuchi (display of active listening)
おじぎ		bowing

Places/Signs

ばしょ	場所	place
ちかてつ	地下鉄	subway
ゆうびんきょく	郵便局	post office
かいしゃ	会社	company
うけつけ	受付	reception desk
あんない	案内	information desk
ひじょうぐち	非常口	emergency
こうつうひょうしき	交通標識	traffic sign
たちいりきんし	立ち入り禁止	off-limits

きんえん	禁煙	no smoking
いっぽうつうこう	一方通行	one way
とまれ	止まれ	stop

Expressions for Letter

げんき	元気	well/healthy
はいけい	拝啓	Dear Sirs:
けいぐ	敬具	Sincerely yours,
ぜんりゃく	前略	*zenryaku* (indicates that greetings are abbreviated)
ひづけ	日付	date
あてさき	宛先	address
さしだしにん	差出人	sender
～ゆき	～行き	to~
～さま	～様	Mr./Mrs./Ms.
～へ		to (someone)
～より		from (someone)/sender

Verbs

のこす	残す	to leave something
つたえる	伝える	to inform
おくる	送る	to send
だす	出す	to send out
かける（でんわ）		to telephone
うつ（でんぽう）	打つ	to send a telegram
つづく	続く	to be continued

 *My Body / My Health*

Beginning Level

Outcomes	Suggested Assessment Activities
1. Student expresses basic health conditions, relating them to parts of the body.	A. After listening to a tape of a dialogue between a patient and doctor, or between friends, student expresses where the pain or problem is. B. After selecting a card illustrating a part of the body (for example, mouth), student responds by expressing what activities he or she does using that body part (I sing; I eat).
2. Student comments on what he or she is feeling or experiencing through the five senses.	A. Given visual cues of facial expressions, student describes the emotion shown. B. After surveying and discussing food likes or dislikes with other students, student describes the flavor and his or her reaction to food made by students.
3. Student uses and understands safety-related terms in emergency situations.	A. Given visual cues (such as a child running after a ball in a street), student responds with an appropriate warning or advice. B. Student listens to directions in Japanese and explains his or her resulting behavior in English (such as not to take the elevator, to turn off the gas, and so on).

Language Components

Context
The human body • How does one express illness, discomfort, or general condition of health? • How does a given culture use idiomatic expressions involving parts of the body to express health or feelings? **Feelings** • What are appropriate ways to express what one is seeing, tasting, hearing, smelling, and touching? • How are emotions expressed in a given culture? • What sights, smells, or tastes evoke images of a place or of a culture? **Healthy living** • What are some routine personal health habits? • What practices promote health and safety in a given culture?

Sample Expressions	Structure
A:どうしましたか。 B:頭が痛いです。	
おなかがすきました。／おなかがすいた。	
のどがかわきました。／のどがかわいた。	
疲れました。／疲れた。	
私も鼻が高いです。	〜も
耳が痛いです。	
黒板がよく見えません。	〜ません／ない
このサンドイッチはおいしいですねえ。	…ねえ
このレモネードはすっぱいですよ。	…よ
となりのステレオがうるさいです。	N の N
あぶない!	
気を付けて!	
手をきれいに洗いましょう。	Adj (na) に
地震の時は、エレベータを使ってはいけません。	〜てはいけない
すぐストーブを消しましょう。	〜ましょう

Transitional Level

Outcomes	Suggested Assessment Activities
1. Student describes and gives an explanation for pain, disease, or injury.	A. Given visual cues or gestures depicting various symptoms, student describes the problem. B. Role-playing a visit to the doctor's office, the student responds to the doctor's questions by describing his or her problem and offering possible reasons.
2. Student expresses concern or sympathy.	A. After picking a card depicting a situation of concern, student responds with an appropriate expression.
3. Student identifies healthy and unhealthy lifestyles.	A. After conducting a survey of health-related habits, student writes a summary, categorizing the results as being healthy or unhealthy. B. Given pictures of food, student states the amount and frequency of consumption that is good for health.
4. Student expresses qualities experienced through the senses.	A. Provided with a sensory stimulus (such as a feather, an ice cube, or tofu), student expresses how it feels, tastes, smells, looks, or sounds (such as it smells good, or it feels soft).

Transitional Level

Language Components

Context
Health and culture • What factors influence the diet of an individual or region? • How does culture affect one's expression of concern or sympathy in health-related situations? • What conditions one's attitude about what constitutes a healthy or unhealthy lifestyle? • What activities are considered healthy in a culture and why? • What factors account for differences of opinion on wellness: age, socioeconomic factors, or culture?

Sample Expressions	Structure
A:どうしたんですか。 B:胃がシクシク痛むんです。	
きのうアイスクリームを食べすぎました。	～すぎる
スケートをしていて転びました。	…て
捻挫したらしいです。	…らしい
雨にぬれたので、かぜをひきました。	…ので…
大丈夫ですか。	
気を付けてくださいね。	～てください
お大事に。	
A: 何か運動していますか。 B: 週に三回プールで泳いでいます。	なにか period of time に#かい
食べ物の好き嫌いがありますか。	～がある
私は野菜が嫌いで、魚もあまり好きではありません。	Adj (na)で
甘いものはあまり食べないほうがいいです。	～ないほうがいい
食べすぎは健康によくないです。	～すぎ
果物は毎日、食べたほうがいいです。	～たほうがいい
アイスクリームは冷たくておいしいです。	Adj (i) stem くて
フワフワして柔らかいです。	
いい匂いですねえ。	Adj (i) + N

Intermediate Level

Outcomes	Suggested Assessment Activities
1. Student identifies purpose and dosage of medicine.	A. After examining a Japanese prescription bag or back of a medicine package, student tells what the medicine is for, the dosage, and frequency to be taken.
2. Student obtains necessary help in an emergency.	A. Shown a picture or role-playing a situation in which an emergency is depicted, student requests assistance from an appropriate person by explaining the emergency. B. Student calls emergency numbers (police, fire department, and ambulance) and asks for help, describing the problem or emergency.
3. Student evaluates environments and individual habits as healthy or unhealthy.	A. In discussion about a solution to a given environmental threat to health, student adds to the description of the problem and suggests a solution. B. Student describes when he or she feels stress and explains how he or she relieves that stress.
4. Student incorporates body-related idioms in daily communication.	A. Students create dialogues in which the last line is an appropriate body-related idiom (for example, the expression "I am pulling your leg," which has totally different meanings in English and Japanese). After each dialogue is presented without the last line, student completes each dialogue by writing down the appropriate body-related idiom.
5. Student identifies health practices similar or different to his or her own.	A. After interviewing a Japanese visitor about health practices in Japan, student writes a brief article on similarities and differences with U.S. health practices.

Intermediate Level

Language Components

Context
Medical practices • How are medical services delivered in a given society? • What attitudes and beliefs affect medical care? • What alternative treatments are practiced? Healthy and unhealthy lifestyles • What factors affect one's physical, mental, or emotional health? • What societal circumstances (positive or negative) affect one's choice of leisure activities or sports?

Sample Expressions	Structure
この薬は頭痛によくききます。	Adj (i) stem く
一日三回食事の後で1錠ずつ飲んでください。	〜のあとで #ずつ
もう薬を飲まなくてもいいです。	〜なくてもいい
切り傷にはこの薬をつけるといいです。	〜といい
病院はどこですか。	どこ
救急車をよんでください。	〜てください
119番です。火事ですか。救急ですか。	…か。…か。
駅やレストランは全て禁煙にするべきです。	…べき
排気ガスを減らすために、なるべく車に乗らないようにしましょう。	…ために 〜ないようにする
宿題が多くて睡眠不足です。	Adj (i) stem くて
テレビゲームをやめて、もっと運動するようにしましょう。	もっと〜ようにする
ジョギングはストレス解消になります。	〜になる
目を丸くしました。	Adj (i) stem くする
はらが立ちました。	
耳が遠いんです。	…んです
かぜは熱いチキンスープを飲むとすぐ治ります。	…と

Advanced Level

Outcomes	Suggested Assessment Activities
1. Student articulates and supports personal opinions on a healthy lifestyle.	A. After reading an article about health-related issues, student supports or opposes the main ideas and explains his or her reasons. B. As student groups present two contrasting opinions on a contemporary topic related to health, each student presents his or her opinion.
2. Student comprehends emergency announcements.	A. Student listens to or watches broadcasts of emergency information and summarizes the events and consequences.
3. Student comprehends prohibitions or warnings.	A. Student matches Japanese signs to their English equivalents. B. Student comprehends signs and follows their directions in order to walk through a maze or complete a flow chart.
4. Student expresses sympathy.	A. Student writes a letter to comfort a sick or injured friend.
5. Student provides personal health history.	A. Given a fictitious medical history, student completes health survey and/or a medical history form.
6. Student describes symptoms and asks for assistance in a pharmacy.	A. Student inquires about appropriate treatment for a given condition or symptom.

Advanced Level

Language Components

Context
Health and the environment ● What personal habits affect health? ● How do people protect themselves in natural emergencies? ● How have natural disasters affected people's lifestyles or attitudes? **Health institutions** ● What institutions and government policies affect and support people's health? ● What health insurance or health services exist? ● What social organizations work to encourage a healthy lifestyle? ● What cultural customs influence selection of cards or gifts for hospital patients?

Sample Expressions	Structure
肉より野菜を食べるほうが健康的だと思います。	…とおもう
私は菜食主義だから肉も魚も食べません。	〜も〜も
自分で料理するのが一番です。	…のがいちばん
煙草をすうと肺ガンになるそうです。	…と〜になる …そうだ
たばこと肺ガンは無関係でしょうか。	む (prefix)
強い雨を伴った大型の台風が今夜関東地方を直撃するもようです。	Relative clause + N
住民の方は直ちに避難してください。	〜てください
「危険!立ち入り禁止。」	
「入るな!」	
「あぶない!良い子はここで遊ばない。」	
一日も早く元気になるように祈っています。	…ように
早く元気になってください。	Adj (na) になる
今までに大きな病気をしたことがありますか。	〜たことがある
三才のとき、はしかにかかりました。	name of illness にかかる
何か薬のアレルギーがありますか。	なにか
どんな健康保険に入っていますか。	どんな
A:頭痛がひどいんですが、眠くならない薬ありませんか。 B:これなら運転しても大丈夫ですよ。	… んですが 〜ても

Vocabulary

Parts of Body

Head/Face/Neck

あたま	頭	head
かみ	髪	hair
かお	顔	face
ひたい（おでこ）	額	forehead
まゆ	眉	eyebrow
め	目	eye
はな	鼻	nose
ほほ（ほっぺた）	頬	cheek
くち	口	mouth
くちびる	唇	lips
は	歯	tooth
した	舌	tongue
あご	顎	chin
のど	喉	throat
くび	首	neck
き	気	mind/energy
せいかく	性格	personality
いき	息	breath

Arms/Shoulders/Hands

じょうはんしん	上半身	upper part of body
かた	肩	shoulder
うで	腕	arm
ひじ	肘	elbow
てくび	手首	wrist
て	手	hand
ゆび	指	finger
おやゆび	親指	thumb
ひとさしゆび	人さし指	index finger
なかゆび	中指	middle finger
くすりゆび	薬指	ring finger
こゆび	小指	little finger
つめ	爪	nail

Trunk

むね	胸	chest
せなか	背中	back
こし	腰	waist
おなか		general area of the stomach
い	胃	stomach
しんぞう	心臓	heart

Lower Parts of Body

かはんしん	下半身	lower part of body
しり	尻	buttocks
あし	足	leg/foot
ひざ	膝	knee
あしくび	足首	ankle

かかと		heel
つまさき	爪先	toe
あしのゆび	足の指	toes

Five Senses

あじ	味	taste
かんしょく	感触	touch
におい	匂	smell
かおり	香り	fragrance
おと	音	sound
こえ	声	voice
いろ	色	color
かたち	形	shape

Illness/Injury/Discomfort

びょうき	病気	illness
けが	怪我	injury
かぜ	風邪	cold
ズキズキ		piercing pain
ドキドキ		sound of heartbeat
シクシク		the way stomach hurts
はきけ	吐き気	nausea
せき	咳	cough
くしゃみ		sneeze
めまい		dizziness
ねつ	熱	fever
こっせつ	骨折	broken bone
ねんざ	捻挫	sprained
ずつう	頭痛	headache
いらいら		nervousness
ふくつう	腹痛	stomachache
はいた	歯痛	toothache
きりきず	切り傷	cut
すりきず	擦り傷	scratch
やけど	火傷	burn
アレルギー		allergy
かふんしょう	花粉症	hay fever

Meals/Food

しょくじ	食事	meals
おべんとう	お弁当	packed lunch
りょうり	料理	cooking/food
カレー		curry
ラーメン		ramen noodle
どんぶりもの	丼物	bowl of rice with toppings
ていしょく	定食	set meal
ごはん	ご飯	cooked rice/meal
おかゆ		soft-boiled rice
うめぼし	梅干し	pickled plum
やさい	野菜	vegetable
くだもの	果物	fruit
にく	肉	meat
さかな	魚	fish
かい	貝	shellfish
めんるい	麺類	noodles

そば		buckwheat noodles
うどん		noodles
ラーメン		Chinese noodles
スパゲティ		spaghetti
チキンスープ		chicken soup
こめ	米	rice
むぎ	麦	wheat
パン		bread
まめ	豆	beans
なっとう	納豆	*natto* (fermented soy beans)
にゅうせいひん	乳製品	dairy product
ぎゅうにゅう／ミルク	牛乳	milk
チーズ		cheese
ヨーグルト		yogurt
かいそう	海草	sea vegetables/plant
のり	海苔	*nori* (a kind of sea vegetable)
しぼう	脂肪	fat
しょくもつせんい	食物繊維	dietary fiber
しょくもつ	食物	food
しょくもつぐん	食物群	food group
のみみず	飲み水	drinking water
びんづめ	瓶詰め	bottled (water)

Nutrition/Healthy Lifestyle

しょくせいかつ	食生活	eating habit
えいよう	栄養	nutrition
バランス		balance
さいしょくしゅぎ	菜食主義	vegetarian
ゆうきさいばい	有機栽培	organic cultivation
てあらい	手洗い	washing hands
はみがき	歯みがき	brushing teeth
はやねはやおき	早寝早起き	early to bed, early to rise
うがい		gargle
きんえん	禁煙	quit smoking
よぼう	予防	prevention

Unhealthy Lifestyle/Food/Drinks

すききらい	好き嫌い	likes and dislikes
へんしょく	偏食	finicky
たばこ	煙草	cigarette
きつえん	喫煙	smoking
さけ／アルコール	酒／アルコール	alcoholic drinks
いんしゅ	飲酒	drinking
かんしょく	間食	snack
のうやく	農薬	agricultural chemical
てんかぶつ	添加物	additive
かがくちょうみりょう	科学調味料	artificial flavoring
ポストハーベスト		post-harvest
すいみんぶそく	睡眠不足	lack of sleep
ストレス		stress
うんどうぶそく	運動不足	not enough exercise

Diet and Exercise

ダイエット		diet
ひまん	肥満	being overweight
カロリー		calories
ふとりすぎ	太りすぎ	too heavy
やせすぎ	痩せすぎ	too thin
うんどう	運動	exercise
ジョギング		jogging
ウォーキング		walking
エアロビックス		aerobics
ラジオたいそう	体操	radio exercises
ジム		gym

Medicine and Cure

やっきょく	薬局	pharmacy
くすりや	薬屋	drugstore
ちりょうほう	治療法	cure
くすり	薬	medicine
しょくぜん	食前	before meals
しょくご	食後	after meals
#かい	#回	# times
#じょう	#錠	# pills
まえ	前	before
あと	後	after
あいだ	間	between

Safety and Emergencies

きゅうきゅうしゃ	救急車	ambulance
119ばん	119番	#119 (emergency number)
かじ	火事	fire
きゅうきゅう	救急	emergency
きんきゅうほうそう	緊急放送	emergency announcement
てんきよほう	天気予報	weather forecast
なだれ	雪崩	avalanche
つなみ	津波	tidal waves
じしん	地震	earthquake
たいふう	台風	typhoon
たつまき	竜巻	tornado
あんぜん	安全	safety
きけん	危険	danger
けんちくげんば	建築現場	construction site
ひなんくんれん	避難訓練	evacuation drill
たちいりきんし	立ち入り禁止	off-limits
らくせきちゅうい	落石注意	falling rocks
ひなん	避難	evacuate

Hospital

にゅういん	入院	being hospitalized
たいいん	退院	released from the hospital
びょうにん	病人	sick person
しゅじゅつ	手術	operation/surgery
けがにん	怪我人	injured person
ゆけつ	輸血	transfusion
けんけつ	献血	blood donation
けつえき	血	blood

けつえきがた	血液型	blood type
かいふく	快復	recovery
おみまい	お見舞	act/item to comfort the sick or injured
はちうえ	鉢植え	potted plant
リボン		ribbon
けんこうほけん	健康保険	health insurance

Descriptors

あまい	甘い	sweet
からい	辛い	spicy
すっぱい	酸っぱい	sour
にがい	苦い	bitter
しおからい	塩辛い	salty
おいしい		tasty/delicious
まずい		bad tasting
こい	濃い	rich
うすい	薄い	thin
かたい	硬い	hard
やわらかい	柔らかい	soft
つるつるした		smooth
ざらざらした		rough
くさい		smells bad
うるさい		noisy/annoying
にぎやか（な）		lively
いたい	痛い	painful
かゆい		itchy
くるしい	苦しい	painful
けんこうてき（な）	健康的（な）	healthy
げんき（な）	元気（な）	well/healthy
あぶない	危ない	dangerous

Verbs

あじわう	味わう	to taste
さわる	触る	to touch
におう		to smell
みえる	見える	to see
きこえる	聞こえる	to hear
たよる	頼る	to depend on
ころぶ	転ぶ	to fall
すりむく	擦りむく	to skin
かわく（のど）	渇く	to get dry (thirsty)
すく（おなか）	空く	to be empty (hungry)
つかれる	疲れる	to be tired
のむ（くすり）	飲む	to take (medicine)
つける（くすり）		to put (medicine)
きく	効く	to be effective
いたむ	痛む	to hurt
ひく		to catch (a cold)
たりる	足りる	enough/sufficient
かたよる	偏る	to lean to
ふとる	太る	to gain weight
やせる	痩せる	to lose weight
みなおす	見直す	to reconsider

ともなう	伴う	to accompany
みまう	見舞う	to visit sick people
なおす	治す	to cure
なおる	治る	to be cured
～すぎる	～過ぎる	excess of action
よくなる	良くなる	to get well
ちょくげきする	直撃する	to hit/strike
りょうりする	料理する	to cook
にる	煮る	to simmer
やく	焼く	to broil
ゆでる	茹でる	to boil
いためる	炒める	to stir-fry
あげる	揚げる	to deep-fry
きる	切る	to cut
むく	剥く	to peel
きざむ	刻む	to chop
まぜる	混ぜる	to mix
オーブンでやく		to bake/roast

Miscellaneous

よさ	良さ（～さ）	good point
えいきょう	影響	influence
ただちに	直ちに	immediately

 *Rites of Passage*

Beginning Level

Outcomes	Suggested Assessment Activities
1. Student expresses appropriate greetings to a friend on special occasions.	A. Student writes a birthday or graduation card to a friend.
2. Student reads and writes short notes, such as an invitation to a celebration or an announcement, in order to gather and give key information.	A. After receiving an invitation written by another student, student answers specific questions related to the invitation (for example, What time is Sachiko's party?).
3. Student expresses thanks.	A. Student writes a thank-you note to a friend for a gift received.

Beginning Level

Language Components

Context
Points of transition • What ceremonies are related to stages of life? • How are educational milestones noted? • What changes in clothing are related to age? • What changes in expected behavior are related to age? • How is aging viewed by the culture?

Sample Expressions	Structure
お誕生日、おめでとうございます。	
ご卒業おめでとうございます。	
誕生パーティーにぜひ来てください。	～てください
場所は、ぼくのうちです。	～は～です N の N
九月十日の三時からです。	time から
好きなカラオケのテープを持ってきてください。	Adj (na) + N
パーティーはいつですか。	いつ
何時からですか。	time から
だれの誕生日ですか。	だれの～
ぜひ、うかがいます。	いく／うかがう
すてきなプレゼントをありがとうございました。	Adj (na) + N
パーティーはとても楽しかったです。	Adj (i) stem かった

Transitional Level

Outcomes	Suggested Assessment Activities
1. Student lists activities he or she is thinking about doing before the age of twenty-five.	A. Given a timeline from now to age twenty-five, student interviews his or her partner and then fills in the timeline to show what the partner plans to do.
2. Student writes a short note of congratulations for some accomplishment or endeavor.	A. Student writes a note to a friend on the occasion of a recital, license in calligraphy or martial arts, driver's license, graduation, passing an exam, or election to office.
3. Student expresses wishes or hopes.	A. Student writes an ema (wish to hang at the shrine to wish for luck on one's entrance exam, for health of a sick friend, for a boyfriend or girlfriend, and so forth).
4. Student describes or imagines how another person felt when various events happened.	A. Given a simple biography, student creates a timeline of that person's life indicating key events and drawing a face to show the emotion that person felt, and describes for the teacher the event and emotion of one point on the timeline.

Transitional Level

Language Components

Context
Transition points in a teenager's life
• How are the end of elementary school, middle/junior high, senior high, and college marked?
• How are educational and occupational decisions made?
• What are the customs, procedures, and expectations for driving in a given culture?
• What are typical dating customs?

Sample Expressions	Structure
A:16才になったら何をするつもりですか。 B:16才になったら運転免許をとります。	〜つもり 〜たら
大学生になったら、大学で日本語を勉強するつもりです。	〜つもり
一年ぐらい留学しようとおもいます。	V うとおもう
25才までに結婚したいと思います。	〜たいとおもう
合格おめでとうございます。	
よく、がんばりましたね。	
病気が早くよくなりますように。	…ように
6才の時一年生になりました。	〜のとき
8才の時自転車をもらいました。	〜をもらう
10才の時ペットの犬が死んで悲しかったです。	〜て

Intermediate Level

Outcomes	Suggested Assessment Activities
1. Student describes in written or oral form the effects of a rite of passage on his or her life.	A. Student describes how events such as obtaining a driver's license, getting married, or getting a summer job affect or will affect his or her life.
2. Student discusses in written or oral form the topic of employment.	A. Given an advertisement for a part-time job, student scans it to determine conditions of employment and then writes a description of this job. B. Student makes a list of "Dos" and "Don'ts" for a U.S. or Japanese teenager during a job interview, such as appropriate and inappropriate dress for a job interview. C. Student expresses what career he or she wants to have and why.
3. Student presents (orally and in writing) his or her qualifications for a specific purpose.	A. Student writes a personal ad looking for a language partner, pen pal, girlfriend, boyfriend, and so forth. B. Student writes or designs a poster or presents a speech advertising him or herself for some elected office (such as class president or student council).
4. Student demonstrates understanding of key biographical and career information.	A. Student reads a simulated-authentic resume and summarizes the important events of that person's life (for example, born in 1950, graduated 1968, married in 1972, entered company in 1970, and so forth). B. Student interviews a guest speaker and writes a simple resume of his or her accomplishments. C. Student predicts his or her own future life and writes a resume of accomplishments.

Intermediate Level

Language Components

Context
Employment • What cultural expectations are placed on students regarding work, such as frequency, manners, and dress? • When and how do students choose a career path? • How do companies recruit and train employees? • How is the role of women changing societal practice? Activities allowed or prohibited to certain age groups • What are the cultural practices, rules, and expectations for activities restricted by age, such as the following: — drinking alcohol. — smoking. — driving (cars, motorcycles, recreational vehicles). — seeing movies and playing games.

Sample Expressions	Structure
運転免許証をとってから、もっと自由な生活ができるようになりました。	〜てから 〜ようになる
大学生になったら一人で生活することになります。	〜ことになる
この仕事は午前五時から午後一時までです。	time から time まで
一時間八百円もらえます。	もらう／もらえる (potential)
朝早く起きなければなりません。	〜なければならない
アルバイトの面接には、Tシャツとジーンズで行ってもいいでしょうか。	〜てもいい
制服を着たほうがいいでしょう。	〜たほうがいい
帽子はかぶらなくてもいいです。	〜なくてもいい
写真に興味があるのでカメラマンになりたいです。	…ので
私はプールで働く資格をもっています。	Relative clause + N
ぼくは柔道が教えられます。	おしえる／おしえられる (potential)
ぼくが生徒会長に選ばれたら制服をなくします。	えらぶ／えらばれる (passive) …たら
1980年に生まれました。	time にうまれる
19才の時日本の高校生と文通をはじめました。	〜のとき
25才までには、きっと結婚しているでしょう。	time までには きっと〜でしょう／だろう

Advanced Level

Outcomes	Suggested Assessment Activities
1. Student describes earlier times and comments on similarities and differences to the present.	A. Student interviews people in the community and summarizes in a written report what life used to be like. B. Student suggests an important milestone in his or her life and comments on similarities or differences compared to those events in another student's life (such as, I was able to drive when I was 16, which is earlier than in Japan. I started to walk when I was 10 months old).
2. Student describes different forms for similar cultural functions in Japan and the U.S.	A. Students present a written or oral report based on research on a cultural function as it is practiced in two cultures (such as funerals, weddings, or births).
3. Student negotiates a difference of opinion.	A. Student role plays a discussion between a parent and a child to establish or change a household rule.
4. Student presents and supports opinions in a discussion.	A. After researching rules or laws affecting teenagers in different countries or regions, student states where he or she would like to live and why.

Advanced Level

Language Components

Context
Transition points in life • How are weddings celebrated? • What are the rituals of funerals and the reasons behind them? • What are the rituals associated with the birth of a child? People's lives determined by their culture • What occupations are unique to a culture? • What hobbies are strongly influenced by a culture? • What type of activities or professions require licenses? • What type of activities or professions require specialized education? • What forms of gender role socialization take place in a culture? Changes over time • How do communities and cultures change? • What cultural elements do not change, or change very slowly?

Sample Expressions	Structure
おじいさんの若いころは、若い男女が二人だけで出かけることはなかったそうです。	…ころ …ことはない
アメリカでは日本より２年早く車の運転ができるようになります。	～より#Adj (i) stem く
子供に名前を付ける時、漢字の意味をよく調べて選びます。	…とき
お葬式は大抵お寺で行われます。	おこなう／おこなわれる (passive)
結婚式は神社でも教会でもかまいません。	～でも ～でも　かまわない
この規則はちょっとおかしいと思います。	～とおもう
どうしてそう思うんですか。	どうして
こちらのほうが正しいのではないでしょうか。	～のではないでしょうか
門限が八時というのはちょっと厳しすぎると思いませんか。	Adj (i) stem すぎる
みんなやってるのに、どうして私だけ駄目なんですか。	…のに
アメリカの十代のほうが、日本より自由があるような気がします。	～ようなきがする

Vocabulary

Birth

たんじょう	誕生	birth
めいめい	命名	to name
せいちょう	成長	growth

Birthday-related Words

たんじょうカード	誕生カード	birthday card
れいじょう	礼状	thank-you letter
しょうたいじょう	招待状	letter of invitation
バースデーケーキ		birthday cake
おしらせ	お知らせ	announcement
じかん	時間	time
ばしょ	場所	place
かいじょう	会場	place where an event takes place
プレゼント／おくりもの	贈り物	present
おみやげ	お土産	gift taken on a visit
おいわい	お祝い	celebration

Childhood Events in Japan and Related Words

ひなまつり	雛祭	*hinamaturi* (Doll Festival)
ひなにんぎょう／おひなさま	雛人形／お雛様	dolls for Doll Festival
こどものひ	子供の日	*kodomonohi* (Children's Day)
こいのぼり	鯉のぼり	*koinobori* (carp-shaped streamer)
しちごさん	七五三	*sichi-go-san*

Employment

アルバイト		part-time job
ぼしゅう	募集	recruitment
おうぼ	応募	application
めんせつ	面接	interview
りれきしょ	履歴書	resume
しゅうしょく	就職	getting job
うんてんめんきょしょう	運転免許証	driver's license
おこづかい	お小遣い	allowance/spending money
にゅうしゃ	入社	entering the company
しかく	資格	qualification
とくぎ	特技	special ability

Feelings

きぼう	希望	hope
よろこび	喜び	joy
かなしみ	悲しみ	sadness
きょうふ	恐怖	fear
こどく	孤独	loneliness

People

こども	子供	child
おとな／せいじん	大人／成人	grown-up/adult
みせいねん	未成年	under age
じゅうだい	十代	teenage

18さいいか	18歳以下	under 18
ろうじん	老人	old people (the elderly)

Weddings

こんやく	婚約	engagement
ゆいのう	結納	formal engagement
けっこん	結婚	marriage
けっこんしき	結婚式	wedding
けっこんひろううえん	結婚披露宴	wedding reception
きょうかい	教会	church
じんじゃ	神社	shrine
おてら	お寺	temple
けっこんしきじょう	結婚式場	wedding hall
しんこんりょこう	新婚旅行	honeymoon
かてい	家庭	home

Funerals

おつや	お通夜	wake
そうしき／こくべつしき	葬式／告別式	funeral ceremony
おこうでん	お香典	money given in sympathy
おくやみ	お悔やみ	condolences
かそうば	火葬場	crematorium
さいじょう	斎場	funeral parlor
おはか	お墓	grave
ぼち	墓地	cemetery
そうぎや	葬儀屋	undertaker/mortician
もふく	喪服	mourning clothes

Descriptors

うれしい	嬉しい	happy
かなしい	悲しい	sad
こわい	怖い	scared
さびしい	寂しい	lonely
きちんとした		tidy/decent
じゆう（な）	自由（な）	free

Verbs

うまれる	生まれる	to be born
そだつ	育つ	to grow up
しぬ	死ぬ	to die
いわう	祝う	to celebrate
はたらく	働く	to work
かせぐ	稼ぐ	to earn
よろこぶ	喜ぶ	to be happy
かなしむ	悲しむ	to be sad
おいのりする	お祈りする	to pray
おねがいする	お願いする	to wish for/desire
かわる	変わる	to change

Schools and Education

Beginning Level

Outcomes	Suggested Assessment Activities
1. Student expresses degrees of preference or dislike for school.	A. Student interviews a classmate about the degree to which he or she likes or dislikes various things about school (such as subjects or homework).
2. Student inquires about an individual's school schedule and describes his or her own schedule.	A. Given a schedule grid to fill in, student interviews a person about his or her class schedule (such as what day of the week and what time are classes).
3. Student reads a simple class schedule (main subjects) to find out key information.	A. Given a Japanese student's schedule of classes, the student responds (orally or in writing) to questions based on its contents.
4. Student gives classroom commands and responds appropriately to commands given by others.	A. Given a visual representing a classroom situation, student says and performs the culturally appropriate command and/or gesture, such as the Japanese attendance procedure. B. Throughout the year, student performs the role of a teaching assistant (such as toban). C. Student completes an origami project according to instructions given by teacher in Japanese.
5. Student gives basic personal identification information.	A. Student writes own nametag (nafuda) or school identification card. B. Student creates own business card (meishi).

Beginning Level

Language Components

Context
Educational systems   • How are the years of formal education divided and grouped?   • What rules or expectations affect student dress and behavior?   • What classes and subjects are offered or required at different ages?   • How are the school day and school year organized?   • What are the responsibilities of students in and out of school?   **Classroom language**   • What are appropriate greetings for teachers and for fellow students?   • What is the attendance procedure?   • What classroom instructions are common?   • Are classrooms more teacher- or student-oriented?

Sample Expressions	Structure
ゆかりさんは理科が好きですか。	〜がすき
理科は好きですが、あまり得意ではありません。	…が、…
理科と数学とどっちが好きですか。	〜と〜とどっちが
どっちもあまり好きじゃありません。	どっちも／どちらも
理科は苦手です。	〜は Adj (na)
どのクラスが一番好きですか。	〜がいちばん Adj
月曜日の1時間目は何のクラスですか。	#じかんめ
先生の名前は何ですか。	N の N
何番の教室ですか。	#ばん
おはようございます。	
失礼します。	
起立、礼、着席	
出席をとります。	
山田さんは欠席ですね。	
田中さんも、お休みです。	〜も
立ってください。	〜てください
座ってください。	
答えてください。	
もう一度言ってください。	

Transitional Level

Outcomes	Suggested Assessment Activities
1. Student makes simple statements describing similarities and differences of education in Japan and the U.S.	A. Using simple sentences, student compiles a short list in Japanese describing what is similar or different about U.S. and Japanese schools or educational systems.
2. Student demonstrates understanding of the location of people or objects.	A. Given a picture of an empty classroom, student draws in the location of various classroom objects and persons found in the classroom according to directions given by teacher or student partner.
3. Student gives and follows verbal and written directions.	A. Given a map of the school, student follows verbal directions and marks on the map the location of the classroom to which the directions lead.
	B. Given a map of the school, student describes how to get from classroom A to classroom B.
	C. Student reads and follows instructions for a test.
4. Student completes a simple form or application in Japanese.	A. Given a simplified version of an identification form or book check-out form, student completes the form by writing name, grade, nationality, address, phone number, age, and so forth.
5. Student inquires about and describes materials needed for each of his or her classes.	A. Given photos of teachers of various subjects in the school, student writes the name of the class and describes materials needed.
6. Student expresses and demonstrates understanding of goals and rules in the classroom.	A. Student writes a list of "dos" and "don'ts" for the classroom.
	B. Student works with a partner to compile a list of group goals for the class or school.
	C. Given written slogans (such as "Let's keep our classroom clean" or "Don't run in the hall"), student places them at appropriate locations around the classroom or school (such as over a wastebasket or exit door).

Transitional Level

Language Components

Context
Schools in Japan and the U.S. ● What practices that appear different in their form are similar in their function? ● Who is responsible for providing school materials, books, or uniforms? ● What factors affect homework and studying habits? ● What role does school serve outside of the classroom? **Finding one's way in a school building** ● What different rooms exist in a school, and how does one give directions? ● What social practices are important to know when visiting a school? **Influences on behavior** ● What limitations are placed on students by society? by school? by family? ● What expectations affect students' lives?

Sample Expressions	Structure
アメリカの高校には制服がありません。	〜には
アメリカの学校にも日本の学校にもスポーツのチームがあります。	〜にも〜にも
日本の学校では生徒が掃除をします。	〜では
給食がありますか。それとも、お弁当を持っていきますか。	…か。それとも…か。
宿題が毎日たくさん出ます。	
机の上にノートがあります。	placeにNがある
先生は黒板の前にいます。	Nはplaceにいる
A: すみません、保険室にいきたいんですけど。 B: まっすぐ行って、右にまがったところです。	〜たいんですけど 〜たところ
次の答えの中で正しいものに丸をつけなさい。	〜のなかで
右と左の言葉を線でむすびなさい。	〜で (by means of)
ここに住所と名前と電話番号を書いてください。	〜と〜と
美術のクラスには油絵の具がいります。	
授業中は静かにすること。	…こと。
宿題を忘れてはいけません。	〜てはいけない
教室をきれいにしましょう。	Adj (na)にする
ろうかを走らないでください。	〜ないでください

Intermediate Level

Outcomes	Suggested Assessment Activities
1. Student expresses and supports an opinion.	A. Imagining that he or she is a teacher, student describes the goals and design of a new course being proposed and then promotes the course through a radio or print ad, or a catalog description.
2. Student identifies essential information, using a dictionary if necessary, to grasp key points about school and education.	A. Given a reading, brochure, or course description guide, student reads questions in Japanese, skims and scans for key information, and writes answers in Japanese.
3. Student describes school culture and major school events in written and oral form.	A. Student designs a poster or brochure advertising his or her own school's big event (such as homecoming, play, or sporting event). B. Student reads a letter from a Japanese pen pal that describes a school event and writes a response to his or her questions on a major U.S. school event.
4. Student talks his or her way out of a difficulty by explaining the problem.	A. Student explains why a book is overdue, damaged, or lost and inquires about the consequences.
5. Student gets someone else to do something.	A. Student role-plays by calling another student, explaining that he or she is ill, and asking the other student to collect assignments for the ill student. B. Student describes to a partner what assistance he or she needs with a school club or event and responds to the partner's objections with reasons why the partner should participate.

Intermediate Level

Language Components

Context
School culture • In what ways are parents involved in schools? • How is discipline defined and maintained? • What role is served by night schools? • What festivals, ceremonies, performances, or sports are common in schools? • What role does testing play in one's education? • How is education viewed by the culture? **School behavior** • How do students show respect and friendliness to each other? • How do students and teachers show respect and friendliness to each other? • What verbal and nonverbal behaviors are appropriate for explaining problems?

Sample Expressions	Structure
このクラスの目標は日本語が話せるようになることです。	〜ようになる
このクラスをとるとテニスがじょうずになります。	…と
学校行事の中で一番好きなことは何ですか。	〜のなかで
文化祭ではいろいろなクラブが研究発表や展示をしたり、コンサートをしたりします。	〜たり〜たりする
アメリカの学校ではホームカミングが一番大きな行事です。	〜では
ホームカミングの時はフットボールの試合があります。	〜のとき
図書館の本を電車の中に置き忘れてしまいました。	〜てしまう
どうすればいいですか。	〜ば
今度から、気を付けてください。	
もうしわけありませんでした。	
宿題があるかどうか聞いてきてください。	…かどうか 〜てくる
文化祭の準備をするので3番教室まで来てください。	…ので
宿題がたくさんあるから行けません。	…から
クラス全員参加することになっています。	〜ことになる

Advanced Level

Outcomes	Suggested Assessment Activities
1. Student gives rationale for a decision regarding his or her future.	A. Student conducts research (in English) to prepare an in-class oral presentation or written summary in Japanese regarding plans after high school graduation.
2. Student expresses and supports an opinion.	A. After preparing written notes in Japanese to support a stand taken on an issue, student presents his or her opinion and responds with further explanations to differing opinions given by other students.

Advanced Level

Language Components

Context
Future plans • What influences one's choice of majors, careers, or occupations? • Do gender, age, or race influence one's opportunities? Discussion processes • What are culturally appropriate behaviors and expressions for sharing one's opinion? • What practices are employed when making collective decisions?

Sample Expressions	Structure
どうしてこの大学を選んだのですか。	どうして
この大学は美しい湖のそばにあり、スポーツがさかんです。	V (stem)、…
この大学は教育学部で有名です。	〜でゆうめい
地方にあるので生活費があまりかかりません。	あまり…ない
働きながら勉強することが出来ます。	〜ながら
遊んでばかりいることには賛成できません。	…ことには
勉強するより遊ぶほうがずっといいと思います。	〜より〜ほうがいい
それは間違っているのではないでしょうか。	〜のではないでしょうか
学生はもっと勉強するべきだと思います。	〜べき

Vocabulary

Stages of Education

ぎむきょういく	義務教育	compulsory education
ようちえん	幼稚園	kindergarten
しょうがっこう	小学校	elementary school
ちゅうがっこう（ちゅうがく）	中学校（中学）	junior high/middle school
こうとうがっこう（こうこう）	高等学校（高校）	high school
#ねんせい	#年生	# th grade
たんきだいがく（たんだい）	短期大学（短大）	junior college
せんもんがっこう	専門学校	vocational college
だいがく	大学	university
せんこう	専攻	major in
だいがくいん	大学院	graduate school
がくしゅうじゅく（じゅく）	学習塾（塾）	cram school
よびこう	予備校	cram school for entrance exam
りゅうがく	留学	studying abroad
じゅけん	受験	taking entrance examination
しんがく	進学	going to school

Subjects

じゅぎょう	授業	class
じかんわり	時間割	timetable/school schedule
かもく	科目	school subject
ひっしゅう	必修	requirement
せんたく	選択	elective
さんすう	算数	arithmetic (elementary school)
すうがく	数学	mathematics
だいすう	代数	algebra
きか	幾何	geometry
りか	理科	science
せいぶつ	生物	biology
かがく	化学	chemistry
ぶつり	物理	physics
ちがく	地学	geology
しゃかいか	社会科	social studies
せいじ	政治	politics
けいざい	経済	economics
れきし	歴史	history
ちり	地理	geography
しんりがく	心理学	psychology
しゃかいがく	社会学	sociology
	地学	geology
こくご	国語	*kokugo* (Japanese as studied in Japanese schools)
がいこくご	外国語	foreign language
えいご	英語	English language
ずこう	図工	arts and crafts
びじゅつ	美術	art (more formal study)
しゅうじ	習字	calligraphy
おんがく	音楽	music
コーラス/がっしょう	コーラス／合唱	chorus
バンド		band

たいいく	体育	physical education
かていか	家庭科	home economics
せいかつか	生活科	living arts (integrated social studies and science)

School-related Activities and Customs

ひるやすみ	昼休み	lunch recess
ほうかご	放課後	after school
やすみじかん	休み時間	recess
ホームルーム		homeroom
クラブかつどう	クラブ活動	club activities
ぶかつどう	部活動	club activities (junior and senior high school)
～ぶ	～部	~club
しあい	試合	match/game
せいそう/そうじ	清掃/掃除	clean up
きゅうしょく	給食	school lunch
しゅくだい	宿題	homework
しけん	試験	test/examination
ちゅうかんしけん	中間試験	midterm examination
きまつしけん	期末試験	final examination
レポート		paper (assignment)
せいとかい	生徒会	student council
もくひょう	目標	goal
こうそく	校則	school rules
いはん	違反	violation
アルバイト		student employment
がくせいしょう	学生証	student identification card
けっせきとどけ	欠席届	excuses for absence (note from parent/guardian)
つうちひょう	通知表	report card
せいとてちょう	生徒手帳	students' handbook
ふぼかい(PTA)	父母会	parent-teacher association
きりつ	起立	rise
れい	礼	bow
ちゃくせき	着席	take seat
しゅっせき	出席	present
けっせき/やすみ	欠席／休み	absent
あいさつ	挨拶	greetings
へんじ	返事	reply
せつめい	説明	explanation
いけん	意見	opinion
たいど	態度	attitude

School Events

がっこうぎょうじ	学校行事	school events
にゅうがくしけん	入学試験	entrance examination
ぶんかさい	文化祭	cultural festival
コンサート		concert
ブラスバンド		brass band
しゅうがくりょこう	修学旅行	field trip
うんどうかい/たいいくさい	運動会／体育祭	sports day
そうりつきねんび	創立記念日	foundation day
にゅうがくしき	入学式	entrance ceremony

そつぎょうしき	卒業式	graduation ceremony
ほたるのひかり	蛍の光	Auld Lang Syne (graduation song)
えんげきさい	演劇祭	drama festival
ホームカミング		homecoming
プロム		junior-senior prom
フットボール		football
マスコット		mascot

School Environment

きょうしつ	教室	classroom
ほけんしつ	保健室	sick room
こうばいぶ	購買部	school store
たいいくかん	体育館	gym
どうじょう	道場	gym for *judo* / *kendo*
としょしつ	図書室	library
しょくいんしつ	職員室	teachers' room
こうどう	講堂	auditorium/theater
かいぎしつ	会議室	conference room
こうもん	校門	school main gate
うんどうじょう／グランド	運動場／グランド	playground
プール		swimming pool
しょくどう/カフェテリア	食堂/カフェテリア	cafeteria
がくせいしょくどう（がくしょく）	学生食堂（学食）	school cafeteria

The Classroom

つくえ	机	desk
いす	椅子	chair
とけい	時計	clock
こくばん	黒板	chalkboard
こくばんふき	黒板ふき	eraser (for chalk)
きょうかしょ	教科書	textbook
ほん	本	book
じしょ	辞書	dictionary
ノート		notebook
ワークブック		workbook
えんぴつ	鉛筆	pencil
ペン		pen
マーカー		marker
クレヨン		crayon
いろえんぴつ	色鉛筆	colored pencil
えのぐ	絵の具	paint
ふで	筆	brush
けしゴム	消しゴム	eraser (for pencil marks)
セロテープ		clear tape
チョーク		chalk
がようし	画用紙	construction paper
けいさんき	計算器	calculator
たいいくかんシューズ	体育館シューズ	gym shoes
うわばき	上履き	inside shoes
ちず	地図	map
まど	窓	window
ドア		door
ゴミばこ	ゴミ箱	wastebasket

なふだ	名札	name tag
ぼうし	帽子	hat/cap
かばん		bag
ランドセル		backpack used by elementary school students
えんぴつけずり	鉛筆削り	pencil sharpener
でんとう	電灯	lights

School Personnel

こうちょうせんせい	校長先生	principal
せんせい／きょうし	先生／教師	teacher
～せんせい	～先生	Mr./Mrs./Miss~
がくせい	学生	student
しょうがくせい	小学生	elementary school student
ちゅうがくせい	中学生	junior high school student
こうこうせい	高校生	high school student
だいがくせい	大学生	university student
ほごしゃ	保護者	guardian
せんぱい	先輩	*sempai*-senior
こうはい	後輩	*kohai*-junior
チアリーダー／おうえんだん	応援団	cheerleader
コーチ		coach
せいとかいちょう	生徒会長	president of student council
クラスだいひょう	クラス代表	class representative

Descriptors

ただしい	正しい	correct/right
まちがった	間違った	wrong

Verbs

かんがえる	考える	to think
べんきょうする	勉強する	to study
れんしゅうする	練習する	to practice
まなぶ	学ぶ	to learn
しらべる	調べる	to do research
ならう	習う	to learn
くりかえす	繰り返す	to repeat
わすれる	忘れる	to forget
かりる	借りる	to borrow
かえす	返す	to give back
なおす	直す	to fix
むすぶ	結ぶ	to connect
つける（てん）	付ける（点）	to grade
きめる	決める	to decide
きょうりょくする	協力する	to cooperate
きょうそうする	競争する	to compete
せつめいする	説明する	to explain
まちがえる	間違える	to make an error

Seasonal Events

Beginning Level

Outcomes	Suggested Assessment Activities
1. Student describes the weather verbally.	A. Given a picture, student describes the weather in the picture. B. Looking at a weather map from the newspaper, student responds to teacher's questions on what the weather is like in given cities.
2. Orally and in writing, student gives the date and name of important seasonal events or holidays in Japan and in the U.S.	A. Given a blank calendar, student responds to a picture or an auditory cue by identifying orally or in writing the name of the event and its date.
3. Student expresses desires of what he or she wants or wants to do.	A. During the Star Festival (Tanabata), student writes what he or she desires on a note and hangs it on a bamboo branch.
4. Student writes a seasonal greeting card.	A. Student designs a card and writes a seasonal greeting on it, such as New Year's greeting or midsummer greeting.

Beginning Level

Language Components

Context
Seasons
• What activities or celebrations are associated with different times of the year?
• What weather characterizes different times of the year?
• How is the topic of weather used in social conversation?
• What natural symbols represent each season?

Sample Expressions	Structure
A:いいお天気ですねえ。 B:ええ、ほんとうに。	…ねえ
A:蒸し暑いですねえ。 B:そうですねえ。	…ねえ
A:寒いですか。 B:ええ、ちょっと。	Adjですか
A:明日の天気はどうでしょうか。 B:たぶん、雨でしょう。	〜はどう
フロリダの天気はどうですか。	〜でしょう／だろう
ひなまつりは何月何日ですか。	NのN
今年のイースターはいつですか。	#がつ#にち
春は花見に行きます。	いつ
クリスマスにスケートがほしいです。	〜にいく
ディズニーランドに行きたいです。	ほしい
明けまして、おめでとうございます。	〜たい
今年もどうぞよろしく。	
暑中お見舞い申し上げます。	
メリークリスマス。	

Transitional Level

Outcomes	Suggested Assessment Activities
1. Student describes (in both oral and written form) activities that are associated with key holidays or seasonal events from both Japan and the U.S.	A. Given a photo of a holiday or seasonal event, or a series of photos, student describes three things he or she does personally to celebrate that event.
2. Student inquires about what to wear or take along for various events or situations and responds to the inquiries of others.	A. Given the prompt of a destination, student uses a set of pictures to describe what he or she plans to wear and take along. B. Hearing from a partner what people in a picture are wearing, student tells where the people are going.
3. Student acts in a gift-giving situation with socially appropriate behavior and language.	A. Student writes a short note to give with a gift on a special occasion and says the appropriate expression when making the presentation (such as for a birthday or Valentine's Day).
4. Student acts in a gift-receiving situation with socially appropriate behavior and language.	A. Prompted by an object or an illustration, student says an appropriate expression when receiving a gift and writes a letter of thanks.

Transitional Level

Language Components

Context
Seasonal events and holidays
• How do people celebrate special seasonal events?
• What behaviors are expected in a given culture for giving and receiving gifts?
• What clothing is needed for different events and climates?
• What holidays are borrowed from other cultures? How are they observed in a new culture?

Sample Expressions	Structure
独立記念日には花火を見たりバーベキューをしたりしました。	には 〜たり〜たりする
感謝祭には家族で集まってごちそうを食べます。	〜て
節分には「鬼は外」と言いながら豆をまきます。	…ながら
お花見には何を持って行きますか。	〜には
スケートに行くときは何がいりますか。	…ときは
ダイビングのときは、ウェットスーツを着て、フィンをつけて、手袋もします。	〜のとき 〜て〜て
いつもお世話になりまして、ありがとうございます。	〜て
つまらないものですが、どうぞ。	
これは母が作ったケーキです。	Relative clause + N
皆さんで召し上がって下さい。	たべる／めしあがる
バレンタインデーに、愛をこめて。	
どうも恐れ入ります。	
先日はおいしいお菓子をいただいて、ありがとうございました。	Adj (na) + N
みんなでおいしくいただきました。	Adj (i) stem く

Intermediate Level

Outcomes	Suggested Assessment Activities
1. Student explains in English one Japanese holiday or seasonal event.	A. Student reads a Japanese pen pal's letter, written in Japanese, and explains in English the cultural context of references to holidays or seasonal events to an American friend or family member.
2. Student explains in Japanese one U.S. holiday or seasonal event.	A. Student explains in Japanese the cultural context of U.S. holidays or seasonal events to a Japanese pen pal. B. Student chooses one U.S. holiday or seasonal event and reports to the class about its cultural context.
3. Student writes haiku showing understanding of the use of kigo (seasonal reference words).	A. Student writes one original haiku and other students guess the season by identifying the kigo.

Intermediate Level

Language Components

Context
Holidays and seasonal events • What are the origins of a holiday or seasonal event?
Haiku • Why are seasonal images so important to haiku? • What is unique about this literary form? • How has haiku become an international literary form?

Sample Expressions	Structure
すっかり冬になって、寒い日が続いていますが、お元気ですか。私は元気です。	〜…て …が
さて、クリスマスのことですが……	〜のこと
では、お元気で。	
雪がひどいですが、風邪をひかないように気をつけてください。	〜ないように
お手紙楽しみに待っています。	〜ている
ご家族の皆さんによろしく。	
ハロウィーンには子供たちは仮装をします。	
そして「トリッカトリート」と言いながら近所の家をまわります。	〜ながら
私も子供の時、近所の家にお菓子を貰いに行きました。	V (stem) にいく
近所の人たちは、子供たちのためにお菓子をたくさん買っておきます。	〜のために 〜ておく
アメリカ人にとって一番大切な祝日は何でしょうか。	〜にとって
俳句には必ず季語がいります。	
たとえば「蝶」は春の季語です。	たとえば…
俳句は世界で一番短い詩だといわれています。	…といわれる
ひらがなの数で数えると5-7-5となります。	〜となる

Vocabulary

Annual Events

しょうがつ	正月	New Year's Day
イースター		Easter
はなみ	花見	*hanami* (flower viewing)
どくりつきねんび	独立記念日	Independence Day
たなばた	七夕	*tanabata* (Star Festival)
おぼん	お盆	*obon* (ancestral worship)
ハロウィーン		Halloween
かんしゃさい	感謝祭	Thanksgiving Day
クリスマス		Christmas
バレンタンデー		Valentine's Day
ホワイトデー		White Day

Japanese National Holidays

しゅくさいじつ	祝祭日		national holidays
せいじんのひ	成人の日	1-15	Coming of Age Day
けんこくきねんび	建国記念日	2-11	Foundation Day
しゅんぶんのひ	春分の日	3-20	Spring Equinox
みどりのひ	緑の日	4-29	Greenery Day
けんぽうきねんび	憲法記念日	5-3	Constitution Day
こくみんのしゅくじつ	国民の祝日	5-4	Peoples' Holiday
こどものひ	子供の日	5-5	Children's Day
けいろうのひ	敬老の日	9-15	Respect for Elders Day
しゅうぶんのひ	秋分の日	9-23	Autumnal Equinox
たいいくのひ	体育の日	10-10	Sports Day
ぶんかのひ	文化の日	11-3	Culture Day
きんろうかんしゃのひ	勤労感謝の日	11-23	Labor Day
てんのうたんじょうび	天皇誕生日	12-23	Emperor's Birthday

Socialization

ねんがじょう	年賀状	New Year's Day card
おとしだま	お年玉	*otoshidama* (money gift for New Year's Day)
しょちゅうみまい	暑中見舞	midsummer greetings
おちゅうげん	お中元	midyear gift
おせいぼ	お歳暮	year-end gift
おかえし	お返し	gift (in return)

Clothes/Equipment

ぼうし	帽子	hat/cap
てぶくろ	手袋	gloves
ゆびわ	指輪	ring
めがね	眼鏡	glasses
サングラス		sunglasses
うでどけい	腕時計	wristwatch
ブーツ		boots
くつ	靴	shoes
くつした	靴下	socks
したぎ	下着	underwear
セーター		sweater
ジャケット		jacket

オーバー		overcoat
スカート		skirt
ズボン		trousers
ブラウス		blouse
ワイシャツ		white shirt
ティーシャツ		T-shirt
ジーンズ		jeans
スーツ		suits
ネクタイ		tie
ワンピース		dress
ドレス		gown/fancy dress
タキシード		tuxedo
きもの	着物	*kimono*
ねまき／パジャマ	寝間着	pajamas
みずぎ	水着	swimsuit
ウェットスーツ		wet suit
フィン		fin
さんそボンベ	酸素ボンベ	oxygen tank

Seasonal Expressions

きせつ	季節	season
さくら	桜	cherry blossoms
つゆ	梅雨	rainy season
はなび	花火	fireworks
こうよう／もみじ	紅葉	autumn color (fall folliage)
はつゆき	初雪	first snow
きご	季語	*kigo* (seasonal expressions used in *haiku*)

Food

おぞうに	お雑煮	special Japanese dish for New Year
ひなあられ	雛あられ	*hina-arare* (sweets for Doll Festival)
かしわもち	柏餅	*kashiwamochi* (sweets eaten on Children's Day)
しちめんちょう／ターキー	七面鳥	turkey
チョコレート		chocolate
キャンディー		candy

Verbs

かぶる		to wear on the head
きる	着る	to wear
はく		to wear (lower parts of body)
ぬぐ	脱ぐ	to take off
する		to put on (gloves)
つける		to put on accessories
もっていく	持って行く	to take along
もらう	貰う	to receive
いただく	頂く	to take/receive (humble form)
あげる		to give
さしあげる	差し上げる	to give (with respect)
くれる		to be given by others
もぐる	潜る	to dive
はめる		to wear (hands/wrists/fingers)

115

Self, Family, and Friends

Beginning Level

Outcomes	Suggested Assessment Activities
1. Student greets others and makes introductions.	A. Student greets and introduces him or herself to the class. B. Given a card that describes a situation, student introduces one individual to another.
2. Student introduces him or herself in a short presentation.	A. Student introduces him or herself, including name, age, year in school, residence, hobbies, birthday, nationality, and so forth. B. Student writes a short letter of self-introduction, answering questions posed by a Japanese pen pal. C. Student completes simple (simulated-authentic) personal data form.
3. Student exchanges personal information with others.	A. After listening to several introductions, student records the information gathered. B. Student interviews classmates, who have been given fictional identities, to gather personal information.
4. Student describes someone he or she knows well.	A. Using a photo for support, student explains the characteristics, talents, and special skills of a family member, friend, or pet.

Beginning Level

Language Components

Context
Self and friends ● What cultural expectations affect how one talks about oneself, including one's abilities? ● What cultural expectations affect how one talks about others, including their abilities? ● Do age and gender affect the choice of language to talk to or talk about others? ● How is self defined? **Families** ● Who comprises the core family? ● Does a hierarchy exist within a family? ● How is contact maintained with the extended family? ● Are pets treated like members of the family?

Sample Expressions	Structure
A: はじめまして。どうぞ、よろしく。 B: こちらこそ。	
ぼくは、青木健太です。	〜は〜です
こちらは林さんです。	〜は〜です
林さんは学校の友達です。	N の N
林さんはテニスがじょうずです。	〜は〜がじょうず
A: お名前は。 B: 青木ゆみ子です。	
ぼくは九才です。	#さい
アメリカ人です。	country+じん
ぼくは四年生です。	#ねんせい
ぼくは横浜に住んでいます。	place にすんでいる
四人家族です。	#にん
ぼくは野球が好きです。	〜は〜がすき
私はなわとびが出来ます。	〜は〜ができる
A: ペットがいますか。 B: ええ、ネコがいます。	〜がいる
A: これは、うちのイヌです。 B: わあ、大きいですねえ。	…ねえ
うちに、白いネコがいます。	Adj (i) + N

Transitional Level

Outcomes	Suggested Assessment Activities
1. Student gives detailed information on his or her family.	A. Using a photo for visual support, student describes the individual members of his or her family, or of a fictitious family. B. Student writes a letter to a Japanese pen pal describing his or her family members in detail, including interests, occupations, appearance, and so forth.
2. Student obtains information about another's family.	A. After listening to descriptions of different families, student identifies photos matching the families. B. Given a photo, student listens to a description of the family and identifies individual family members described. C. Student interviews classmates about their families and records the information on a chart.
3. Student expresses dreams or goals for the future.	A. Students work in pairs, interviewing one another about their goals for the future. Based on the notes taken during the interview, student writes a summary of his or her partner's goals or dreams. Student then reads the summary to the class for members to guess to whom the summary refers. Questions related to travel, residence, family, employment, and education may be included.

Transitional Level

Language Components

Context
Families ● How does one address family members in different cultures? ● What expressions are appropriate for talking about family members? **Future goals** ● Who or what influences decisions about future career choices or goals?

Sample Expressions	Structure
父は背が高くてやせています。	Adj (i) stem くて
兄は父より背が高いです。	～より Adj
母は水泳が大好きで、毎日プールで泳ぎます。	Adj (na)で
父の仕事は消防士です。	NのN
妹の好きなことはテレビゲームです。	…こと
日曜日は家族で散歩したり買い物に行ったりします。	～たり～たりする
A:兄弟がいますか。 B: 姉が二人と、弟が一人います。	～が#いる
大人になったら、どんな仕事をしたいですか。	…たら ～たい
いつか日本に行きたいですか。	いつか

Intermediate Level

Outcomes	Suggested Assessment Activities
1. Student summarizes information about an individual.	A. Student writes an article about a person after listening to or reading an extensive interview describing that individual. B. After listening to a physical description of an individual, student identifies the person described. C. After listening to a description of an individual's actions, student identifies the person described.
2. Student exchanges information about family rules and routines.	A. Student makes a list of what is permitted or forbidden for a Japanese student staying at his or her home. B. Student writes statements comparing or contrasting his or her family's rules with those of another family (U.S. or Japanese).
3. Student describes the chores and household responsibilities of family members.	A. After completing a reading or watching a video on family life in another country, student lists cultural observations.
4. Student makes and supports a decision based on information gathered through reading.	A. After reading several personal profiles, student chooses the person he or she would like to correspond with and explains that choice.
5. Student describes a past experience, including his or her reaction to that experience.	A. Student writes or tells about an event involving family or friends, and explains how he or she felt at the time.

Intermediate Level

Language Components

Context
Observations on families • What are the differing responsibilities of family members? • What are the differing roles of family members? **Routines in a home and family** • What rules exist in one's home and family? • What suggestions would be helpful to a visitor to one's home?

Sample Expressions	Structure
田中さんは髪が長いです。	〜は〜が Adj (i)
林さんは背が高くてハンサムで、めがねをかけています。	Adj (i) stem くて/Adj (na) で
山田さんはあそこで新聞を読んでいる人です。	Relative clause + N
うちの門限は八時です。	〜は〜です
遅くなる時は電話をしなくてはなりません。	…とき 〜なくてはならない
テレビを見ながらごはんを食べてはいけません。	…ながら 〜てはいけない
家の中では靴を脱がなくてもいいです。	〜なくてもいい
私は妹のめんどうをみたりペットの世話をしたりします。	〜たり〜たりする
妹はよく家の手伝いをします。	
私は明るい性格で、スポーツが大好きです。	…で
友達になってください。	〜てください
クリスマスには姉が帰ってくるから楽しみです。	〜てくる …から
でも、みんな帰ったあとは寂しくなります。	〜たあと Adj (i) stem くなる

Advanced Level

Outcomes	Suggested Assessment Activities
1. Student compares his or her family life to that of a person from another culture.	A. Student writes a composition comparing his or her family life to that of a person from another culture. B. Student reads about family life in another culture and answers questions from the teacher or other students regarding similarities and differences with his or her own culture.
2. Student states an observation of another's emotional condition and hypothesizes the cause of that emotion.	A. Given a picture of someone in an emotional state (such as someone crying), student guesses what may have happened and shares this with another student or the teacher.
3. Student gives advice to resolve a problem.	A. After picking a card describing a situation or problem, student offers advice.
4. Student describes the act of giving and receiving between individuals who are related in various ways.	A. Given a visual depicting a variety of giving and receiving situations between individuals of various ages and status, student describes the situation, mentioning both the giver and the recipient of the item. B. Given a visual depicting various favors done between two individuals of various ages and status, student describes the situation, mentioning both the giver and recipient of the favor.
5. Student defines what a particular term or concept means to him or her.	A. Student writes a descriptive paragraph specifying the qualities found in an ideal friend.

Language Components

Context
Personal experiences
• What is the range of diversity in families?
• What are the customs and expectations for giving and receiving gifts?
• On what occasions are gifts expected, and by whom?
• How do different cultures define and value friendships?

Sample Expressions	Structure
どんなところが同じで、どこがちがいますか。	…で
お父さんがよく家事を手伝うところが私の家族と違う点です。	…ところ
あの人は泣いているようですね。	… ようだ
どうしたんでしょうね。	〜んでしょう
とても嬉しそうですね。	Adj (i) stem そう
たぶん好きな人から返事がきたのでしょう。	たぶん…のでしょう
何かいいことがありましたか。	なにか
A: 母と喧嘩ばかりして困っています。 B: お母さんとよく話し合ったらどうですか。	〜ばかり 〜たらどう
おじいさんが私に入学祝をくれました。	くれる
私はお正月に両親からお年玉を貰いました。	someone から N をもらう
私は友達にプレゼントを上げました。	someone に N をあげる
校長先生から記念品をいただきました。	someone から N をいただく
おばあさんの荷物を持ってあげました。	〜てあげる
私にとって「いい友達」とは悪いことは悪いと言ってくれる人です。	〜てくれる Relative clause + N
私の考える「いい友達」というのは、何でもわかってくれる友達です。	〜というのは
困ったときは、いつも親友に助けてもらいました。	…とき 〜てもらう

Vocabulary

Personal Information

なまえ	名前	name
ねんれい	年齢	age
じゅうしょ	住所	address
でんわばんごう	電話番号	phone number
#がくねん	#学年	grade #
#くみ	#組	class #
しゅみ		hobby
せいねんがっぴ	生年月日	date of birth
たんじょうび	誕生日	birthday
すきなこと	好きなこと	things I like
とくいなこと		things I am good at

Pets

ペット		pet
イヌ	犬	dog
ネコ	猫	cat
モルモット		guinea pig
ハムスター		hamster
ハツカネズミ		mouse
ウサギ		rabbit
カメ		turtle
ヘビ		snake
カメレオン		chameleon
ことり	小鳥	birds
インコ		parakeet
カナリア		canary
きんぎょ	金魚	goldfish
ねったいぎょ	熱帯魚	tropical fish
カブトムシ		giant beetle
かいぬし	飼い主	owner

Personal Relationship

じぶん	自分	self
わたし	私	I (girl/adult)
ぼく		I (boy/young man)
たにん	他人	others/stranger
ともだち	友	friend
しんゆう	親友	best friend
どうきゅうせい／クラスメート	同級生	classmate
なかのいいともだち／なかよし	仲の良い友達／仲良し	good friend
ともだちどうし	友達同士	being a friend to each other
おさななじみ	幼馴染み	childhood friend
ペンフレンド		pen pal
ガールフレンド		girlfriend
ボーイフレンド		boyfriend
こいびと		sweet heart
こんやくしゃ／フィアンセ	婚約者	fiancee or fiance
～さん		Miss/Mr./Mrs./Ms.
～くん	君	address used for boys
～ちゃん		used with the first name

Family and Relations

かぞく	家族	family
おや	親	parent
りょうしん	両親	parents
こども	子供	children
ようし	養子	adopted child
きょうだい	兄弟	brothers and sisters
むすめ	娘	daughter
むすこ	息子	son
おとうさん／ちち	お父さん／父	father
おかあさん／はは	お母さん／母	mother
おにいさん／あに	お兄さん／兄	older brother
おねえさん／あね	お姉さん／姉	older sister
いもうと	妹	younger sister
おとうと	弟	younger brother
あかちゃん	赤ちゃん	baby
しんせき	親戚	relatives
おじいさん／そふ	お祖父さん／祖父	grandfather
おばあさん／そぼ	お祖母さん／祖母	grandmother
おじさん／おじ	叔父／伯父	uncle
おばさん／おば	叔母／伯母	aunt
めい	姪	niece
おい	甥	nephew
いとこ	従姉妹／従兄弟	cousin

Married Relationship

けっこん	結婚	marriage
りこん	離婚	divorce
さいこん	再婚	second marriage
おっと/しゅじん	夫／主人	husband (a, the, my)
つま／かない	妻／家内	wife (a, the, my)
ごしゅじん	ご主人	another's husband
おくさん	奥さん	another's wife

Feelings

きもち	気持ち	feelings
かんじょう	感情	emotion
すき	好き	like
きらい	嫌い	dislike
あい	愛	love
あいじょう	愛情	affection
にくしみ	憎しみ	hatred
かわいそう		pitiful

Hair Style

かみがた	髪形	hairstyle
ロングヘア		long hair
ショートカット		short hair
まるがり	丸刈	close-clipped hair (crew cut)
パーマ		permed
ストレート		straight

Hair Color

かみのいろ	髪の色	hair color
くろかみ	黒髪	black hair
くりいろ	栗色	dark brown
きんぱつ	金髪	blond
あかげ	赤毛	redhead
しらが	白髪	gray hair

Hobbies

カラオケ		*karaoke*
どくしょ	読書	reading
えんげい	園芸	gardening
しゅげい	手芸	craft
さんぽ	散歩	taking a walk
とざん	登山	mountain climbing
え	絵	painting
しゃしん（カメラ）	写真	photography
おんがくかんしょう	音楽鑑賞	music appreciation
コンサート		concert
ご	碁	*go*
しょうぎ	将棋	*shogi*
チェス		chess
えんげき	演劇	drama/theater
えいが	映画	movie
しゅうじ	習字	calligraphy
え	絵	drawing/painting
すみえ	墨絵	*sumie*
はいく	俳句	*haiku*
りょこう	旅行	traveling
ドライブ		driving
スポーツ		sports

Occupation

しょくぎょう／しごと	職業／仕事	occupation/work
きょうし	教師	teacher
かしゅ	歌手	singer
いしゃ	医者	doctor
はいしゃ	歯医者	dentist
かんごふ／かんごし	看護婦／看護士	nurse/male nurse
べんごし	弁護士	lawyer
しょうぼうし	消防士	firefighter
けいさつかん	警察官	police officer
がいこうかん	外交官	diplomat
コンピュータプログラマー		computer programmer
システムエンジニア		system engineer
エンジニア		engineer
じえいぎょう	自営業	self-employed
のうぎょう	農業	agriculture/farming
らくのう	酪農	dairy farming
うんてんしゅ	運転手	driver
じゅうい	獣医	veterinarian
びようし	美容師	hair stylist
しゅふ	主婦	homemaker
だいがくきょうじゅ	大学教授	professor

でんきぎし	電気技師	electrician
だいく／けんせつぎょう	大工／建設業	carpenter/builder
いりょうぎじゅつしゃ	医療技術者	medical technician
かいけいし	会計士	accountant
すいどうや	水道屋	plumber
しゅうりや	修理屋	repairer
りょうりにん	料理人	cook
しょうけんマン	証券マン	stockbroker
セールスマン		salesperson
ぎんこういん	銀行員	bank employee
かいしゃいん	会社員	company employee
としょかんいん／ししょ	図書館員／司書	librarian

Household Chores/Rules

てつだい	手伝い	help
そうじ	掃除	clean-up
くつみがき	靴磨き	polishing shoes
おつかい	お使い	running an errand
ゴミだし	ごみ出し	taking garbage out
みずやり	水やり	watering (plants)
ゆきかき	雪かき	shoveling snow
もんげん	門限	curfew
せわ	世話	taking care of (pets, family)

Descriptors

にどめの	二度目の	the second
じつの	実の	real (biological)
ぎりの	義理の	~in law
したしい	親しい	close
せがたかい	背が高い	tall
せがひくい	背が低い	short
やせている	痩せている	thin
ふとっている	太っている	fat
かわいい	可愛い	pretty/cute
おとなしい		quiet
きびしい	厳しい	strict
やさしい	やさしい	gentle/kind
こわい	怖い	scary
にこにこしている		smiling

Verbs

はなしあう	話し合う	to discuss
つとめる	勤める	to work for an organization
かける（めがね）		to wear (glasses)
てつだう	手伝う	to help/assist
なく	泣く	to cry
わらう	笑う	to laugh/smile
あいする	愛する	to love
にくむ	憎む	to hate
あわれむ	哀れむ	to feel pity for
こまる	困る	to be annoyed
めいわくする	迷惑する	to be troubled by
できる	出来る	to be able to/can do

 *Shopping*

Beginning Level

Outcomes	Suggested Assessment Activities
1. Student writes a simple shopping list based on a specific situation.	A. Given a situation (such as buying back-to-school supplies, going on a field trip, preparing a lunch, or having a birthday party), student creates a list of items needed.
2. Student communicates interest and disinterest in various items through a combination of verbal and nonverbal communication.	A. After bringing items to class, student role-plays either the vendor or customer and uses Japanese currency. Teacher might also create a Japanese store using authentic products from Japan.
3. Student inquires, confirms, and reacts to pricing and the relative value of items.	A. Student questions the teacher about the prices of various items, records the prices, and then judges whether such a price is inexpensive, typical, or expensive for such an object.
4. Student confirms availability and location of an item for purchase.	A. Student role-plays a customer asking several businesses or store clerks about the availability and location of a particular item.

Beginning Level

Language Components

Context
Making purchases ● What behaviors and expressions are commonly employed when making purchases in different cultures? ● How generic or specialized are stores in different countries? ● How are items located in different stores? ● How is value calculated with differing exchange rates?

Sample Expressions	Structure
本とノートと鉛筆と消しゴムがいります。	〜と〜と〜と〜
いらっしゃいませ。	
このガムはいくらですか。	この〜
これを下さい。	〜をください
まいど、ありがとうございます。	
A: これは五万円です。 B:わあ、高いですねえ。	#えん Adjですねえ
A:すみません。テープありますか。 B:すみません。テープはないんですけど。	ある …けど
A:あのう、おもちゃ売り場はどこですか。 B:三階です。	どこ #かい

Transitional Level

Outcomes	Suggested Assessment Activities
1. Student seeks and follows directions to make a desired purchase.	A. Given a picture cue, student asks where the pictured items can be purchased and how to get there, and records the answers on a street, store, or mall map.
2. Student recognizes signs and symbols to determine information on stores.	A. Student answers questions about a variety of business signs regarding the type of business or service, hours of operation, and so forth.
3. Student requests varying quantities of an item and determines the purchase price.	A. Given a Japanese newspaper ad showing various items with prices, student role-plays a customer and identifies how many of an item he or she desires. The partner role-plays a store clerk and replies how much that quantity will cost.
4. Student makes arrangements for purchases to be mailed or delivered (in person and by phone).	A. Student role-plays ordering a service or item for delivery, such as soba, ramen, pizza, concert tickets, or clothing. Student must confirm price, time, and location of delivery.
5. Student identifies the relative value of Japanese currency.	A. Given two ads, one priced in dollars and one in yen, student determines the less expensive of the two items. B. Student records and reports the daily yen-to-dollar exchange rate over the course of a month or the monthly rate over the year. Student then discusses the impact of any changes for purchasing age-appropriate items (such as CDs, toys, comic books, or cars).

Transitional Level

Language Components

Context
Different stores and shops • What kinds of stores exist in different countries? • What kinds of items do they carry? • How frequently do people do their grocery shopping? • How do people make purchases in small stores? • Who usually does the shopping for a family? **Purchases from your home** • How common and convenient is shopping by telephone? • Are mail-order catalogues a part of every culture?

Sample Expressions	Structure
ウォークマンがほしいんですが、どこで売っていますか。	…んですが
秋葉原へは、どう行ったらいいですか。	…たらいい
地図をかいてくれませんか。	～てくれませんか
何時から何時までですか。	time から time まで
日曜日でもあいていますか。	～でも
木曜日は休みです。	～は
このノートは一冊いくらですか。	～は# (1)いくら
このノートを三冊ください。	～を#ください
この本は二冊で三百円です。	～で (totalizing)
Tシャツ三枚と本二冊でいくらですか。	～#と～#で
配達をたのみたいんですが。	～たいんですが
自宅までとどけてください。	place まで
この住所へ送ってください。	～へ
出前お願いできますか。	
六時半までに届けてください。	time までに
三十分以内にお届けします。	#いない
今日は1ドル、#円です。	
このCDはアメリカでは#ドルですが、日本では#円です。	～では…が、～では…

Intermediate Level

Outcomes	Suggested Assessment Activities
1. Student states need, expresses opinions, asks for alternatives, and obtains what he or she wants when shopping.	A. Student role-plays a teacher-designed shopping situation where there is a problem with the item he or she wants to purchase (such as the item is out of stock) or has purchased (such as it does not fit).
2. Student demonstrates comprehension of honorific expressions in authentic situations.	A. Student listens to public announcements from a department store or train and identifies key messages.

Intermediate Level

Language Components

Context
Shopping habits • What is the culturally appropriate manner to make a purchase? • How are arrangements made over the phone? • What unique language is used in paging someone?

Sample Expressions	Structure
ちょっと大きすぎますねえ。	Adj (i) stem すぎる
ほかのサイズ（色）がありますか。	
青いのがいるんですが。	Adj (i) の
これは何で出来ているんですか。	～でできている
着てみてもいいですか。	～てみる ～てもいい
これはちょうどいいと思います。	～とおもう
もう少し安いのはありませんか。	Adj (i) の
来週までにほしいんですが。	time までに
この青いのにします。	～にする
大きいのと取り替えてもらえますか。	～てもらう／もらえる (potential)
お客様のお呼び出しを申し上げます。	いう／もうしあげる
いらしゃいましたら一階の受け付けまでおこしくださ い。	お V ください
迷子のご案内を申し上げます。	
お近くのお電話までご連絡ください。	～まで

Advanced Level

Outcomes	Suggested Assessment Activities
1. Student uses Japanese to market or promote a product or service.	A. Student works in a small group to promote a product or service through a printed ad or video commercial.
2. Student compares and contrasts consumer customs and behaviors across cultures.	A. After reading an authentic newspaper or magazine article on statistics of consumer customs and behaviors (such as how much money is spent on a wedding in Japan), student writes a summary and reaction to the content. The article may need to be modified to match student's reading level.

Advanced Level

Language Components

Context
Advertisements
• What cultural differences exist in advertising?
• Are there cultural differences in consumer preferences and expectations?
• What is the frequency of shopping in different cultures and with different age groups?
• What accounts for different attitudes toward credit or cash transactions?

Sample Expressions	Structure
品質がよくて値段が安いからお買い得です。	Adj (i) stem くて …から
今買うと、ナイフのセットがついてきます。	…と
こんなにいい品物がなぜこの値段で出せるのでしょうか。	だす／だせる (potential)
生産地から直接仕入れたので安いんです。	…ので
信じられないようなお値段です。	V (potential) ないような
売り切れないうちに、ぜひどうぞ。	〜ないうちに
クレジットカードの使いすぎが問題になっているようです。	…ようだ
個人小切手は、日本ではあまり使われていません。	つかう／つかわれる (passive)
たいてい、現金かカードで支払います。	〜で (by means of)
日本では結婚式に何百万円もかかるそうです。	＃も …そうだ
日本人はアメリカ人ほど、食料品を一度にたくさん買いません。	〜は〜ほど…ない

Vocabulary

Buying/Selling

かいもの	買い物	shopping
しょうひん	商品	merchandise
ゆにゅうひん	輸入品	imported product
こくさんひん	国産品	domestic product
しょくりょうひん	食料品	food items
しなもの	品物	article/goods
カメラ		camera
ウォークマン		walkman
ふろしき		*furoshiki* (wrapping cloth)
チケット		ticket
おかいどく	お買い得	good price
ねだん	値段	price
ひんしつ	品質	quality
サイズ		size
いろ	色	color

Ordering/Delivering

こうこく	広告	advertisement
テレフォンショッピング		telephone shopping
つうしんはんばい	通信販売	mail-order shopping
つうはんカタログ	通販カタログ	catalog
でまえ	出前	food ordered from home
はいたつ	配達	delivery
ちゅうもん	注文	order
よやく	予約	to book/reserve
ゆうびん	郵便	mail
どうふう	同封	enclosed
ゆうそう	郵送	delivered by mail
へんしんよう	返信用	for return mail
たっきゅうびん	宅急便	home-delivered
けん	県	prefecture
しゅう	州	state
し	市	city
とおり	通り	street
ばんち	番地	street number

Places

プレイガイド		ticket center
スーパー		supermarket
デパート		department store
しんかん	新館	annex (new)
あんない	案内	information desk
うりば	売り場	sales counter
たな	棚	shelf
#かい	#階	# floor
じたく	自宅	one's own house

Events

フリーマーケット		flea market
コンサート		concert

りょこう	旅行	traveling
バーゲンセール		bargain sale

Means of Payment

クレジットカード		credit card
こぎって	小切手	check
げんきん	現金	cash
げんきんかきとめ	現金書き留め	registered mail for cash
ふりかえ	振替	postal transfer
ぎんこうふりこみ	銀行振込	payment through bank account

Public Announcement

おきゃくさま	お客様	customer
およびだし	お呼び出し	paging
まいご	迷子	lost child
ごあんない	ご案内	announcement
お／ご〜	御〜	*o/go〜* (honorific prefix)
れんらく	連絡	contact

Descriptors

めずらしい	珍しい	rare
ていねい（な）	丁寧（な）	polite

Verbs

はらう	払う	to pay
しはらう	支払う	to make payment
ちゅうもんする	注文する	to order
かう	買う	to buy
うる	売る	to sell
たのむ	頼む	to ask/order/request
おくる	送る	to send
とどける	届ける	to deliver
こうかんする	交換する	to exchange

Miscellaneous

ちょくせつ	直接	directly
ぶっか	物価	cost of living
けっこう	結構	nice
しょうひしゃ	消費者	consumer
ぜんぶ	全部	all/total
〜いない	〜以内	within~
かんしゃ	感謝	appreciation

 *Travel and Transportation*

Beginning Level

Outcomes	Suggested Assessment Activities
1. Student describes a simple travel itinerary.	A. Given a point of origin and destination, student describes where, how, when, and with whom one would logically travel there. B. Given a detailed travel itinerary in English, student orally reports the highlights of the itinerary in Japanese to a non-English speaking Japanese visitor. Student includes point of origin, destination, date, departure time, mode of transportation, duration of trip, and so forth.
2. Student gathers essential information from spoken Japanese.	A. Given a blank one-week daily planner calendar, student records the key travel information relayed by instructor or tape regarding an upcoming trip, including departure and arrival times, origin and destination, and mode of transportation. B. In response to oral questions (for example, Where can you exit this station?), student selects the appropriate sign from among many various signboards to provide the information requested.

Beginning Level

Language Components

Context
Modes of transportation • What common means of transportation are used in an area? • What means of transportation do various segments of the population use for daily commutes? Vacation • What are popular destinations for vacations? What makes them popular? • What means of transportation is commonly used when going on a vacation? • With whom are vacations spent?

Sample Expressions	Structure
A:うちから学校まで何でいきますか。 B:たいてい、バスで行きます。	place から place まで、 〜で (by means of)
ときどき、歩いて行きます。	〜て
A:どのぐらいかかりますか。 B:三十分ぐらいです。	#ぐらい
毎日、七時半にうちを出ます。	time に place をでる
八時ごろ学校に着きます。	time ごろ
A: 夏休みにどこかへ行きますか。 B: 京都へ行きます。	どこか place へ／にいく
A:だれと行きますか。 B:友だちと新幹線で行きます。	だれと someone と
この駅の出口はどこですか。	N の N
南口であいましょう。	placeで

Transitional Level

Outcomes	Suggested Assessment Activities
1. Student determines an appropriate travel activity based on specific criteria.	A. Given simulated authentic material (such as a travel brochure), student skims and scans for relevant information needed to plan a trip. Student then reports on the trip selected based on personal preference or predetermined criteria, such as budget or time constraints.
2. Given oral cues, student navigates his or her way to a desired destination.	A. Given oral instructions in Japanese, student takes notes in English and then sketches a rough map to the destination, filling in landmarks mentioned. B. Given a sheet of various kanji used in travel, student identifies the appropriate kanji in response to a situation described orally (for example, You need to find the bank).
3. Student describes a trip in written form.	A. Student writes a postcard to Japanese teacher or Japanese host family about his or her trip. B. Student writes about a trip in journal format.
4. Student exchanges plans with another person for a proposed trip.	A. After interviewing another student about what he or she wants or intends to do, see, and experience on a planned trip, student reports the information in oral or written form.
5. Student requests assistance with travel needs and demonstrates understanding of the essential information given.	B. Given a card with a task, present location, and destination, student asks for help, says where he or she is going, asks clarifying questions, and records information in English to verify that essential information was understood.

Language Components

Context
Traveling
• What supplies are needed for taking a trip?
• What destinations of interest are in an area?
• What activities are popular at different travel destinations?
• What information is needed for taking a trip?
• How much vacation time is typical for various segments of the society?

Sample Expressions	Structure
東京から京都まで二万円ぐらいかかります。	
京都は古いお寺や京都タワーで有名です。	～や～でゆうめい
私は古い建物が好きだから京都へ行きたいです。	…から
駅の前にバス乗り場があります。	place に～がある
学校の前でバスをおりてください。	place で
私のうちは学校のとなりです。	～のとなり
今、箱根に来ています。	きて／いっている
今日はフェリーに乗ったりハイキングをしたりしました。	～たり～たりする
夏休みに家族で旅行に行くつもりです。	～つもり
九州に行こうと思っています。	Vうとおもう
キャンプをするのでテントを持っていきます。	…ので
おみやげはどこで買えますか。	かう／かえる (potential)
京都発の新幹線は5番線ですね。	…ね
この列車は特急券がいりますか。	
博物館に行きたいんですが地図をかいてくれませんか。	…んですが ～てくれませんか

Intermediate Level

Outcomes	Suggested Assessment Activities
1. Student gives and understands explicit directions.	A. After picking a destination card and looking at a map, student writes a memo in Japanese that provides directions to the destination for another student. B. Student receives another student's prepared memo and, not knowing the final destination, traces the route.
2. Student explains all preparations necessary for an extended trip.	A. Student makes a detailed list of what must be done six months ahead of a planned trip, three months ahead, one month ahead, two weeks ahead, one week ahead, and the day before.
3. Student makes a presentation of an actual trip taken.	A. Student brings trip photos to class and presents the trip to classmates orally or through a poster with photos and captions.

Language Components

Context
Trips around the world • What are some regional differences within a given country? • What is the historical background of different regions of Japan? • Why is travel away from home encouraged or discouraged? • What social factors influence choice of transportation?

Sample Expressions	Structure
まず、北へまっすぐ行ってください。	まず
次に、二番目の角を曲がります。	place を V
橋を渡ってまっすぐ行くと右側に学校があります。	…と
方角を間違えないように気を付けましょう。	～ないように
六カ月前にパスポート用の写真をとります。	period of time まえに
前日までにスーツケースを用意します。	time までに
ホームステイの場合はお土産を買っておきます。	～ておく
これは富士山に登ったときの写真です。	…ときの N
日本では、旅行したり買い物したりしました。	～たり～たりする
日本の地理や歴史について少し学びました。	～について

Advanced Level

Outcomes	Suggested Assessment Activities
1. Student uses historical and geographical background of an area to be visited in order to state a rationale for a trip.	A. Working in a small group, student designs a trip and creates a brochure with appropriate historical and geographical background information.
2. Student makes trip-related purchases (such as souvenirs or meals), investigating options, and asking about their historical or regional significance.	A. Student writes questions to make an informed purchase, asking about availability, use, origin, connection to the region, and appropriateness for the purchaser, and records the answers.

Advanced Level

Language Components

Context
Planning a trip • What are the historical, economic, geographic, and social differences between various regions? • What variety in accommodations is available in different regions? • What transportation options exist for traveling in different regions? • What souvenirs or products are unique to different regions? What are they made of? What is their purpose?

Sample Expressions	Structure
この城は歴史的に有名なところです。	
この建物は八世紀に建てられました。	たてる／たてられる (passive)
世界で一番古い木造建築だと言われています。	…といわれている
泊まるところはホテルがいいですか。それとも民宿がいいですか。	…か、それとも…か
特産品にはどんな物がありますか。	〜には
何で出来ていますか。	〜で（できている）
これには何か特別の意味がありますか。	なにか
何のための物ですか。	〜のための N

Vocabulary

Places

うち		home/house
えき	駅	station
あんないじょ	案内所	information desk
いりぐち	入り口	entrance
でぐち	出口	exit
ひがしぐち	東口	east exit
にしぐち	西口	west exit
みなみぐち	南口	south exit
きたぐち	北口	north exit
ちゅうおうぐち	中央口	central exit
くうこう	空港	airport
たてもの	建物	building
おてら	お寺	temple
じんじゃ	神社	shrine
タワー		tower
こうえん	公園	park
びじゅつかん	美術館	art museum
はくぶつかん	博物館	museum
みち	道	street
かど	角	corner (outside)

Modes of Transportation

バス		bus
タクシー		taxi
でんしゃ	電車	train
ちかてつ	地下鉄	subway
くるま	車	car
じてんしゃ	自転車	bicycle
オートバイ		motorcycle
しんかんせん	新幹線	*shinkansen* (bullet train)
ひこうき	飛行機	airplane
あるいて	歩いて	on foot (walking)

Train-related Terms

～はつ	～発	leaving～
～ちゃく	～着	arriving at～
～ゆき	～行	bound for～
れっしゃ	列車	car (train)
#ばんせん／プラットホーム	#番線	platform #
#ごうしゃ	#号車	car #
#ばん	#番	number # (seat)
#ばんめ	#番目	#th
とっきゅうけん	特急券	limited express ticket
していけん	指定券	reserved seat ticket
ふつうれっしゃ	普通列車	local train
きゅうこう	急行	express train
きっぷ	切符	ticket

Time/Duration

なつやすみ	夏休み	summer vacation
#かげつまえ	#力月前	# months ahead of time
ちり	地理	geography
ちりじょう	地理上	geographically
こうげん	高原	plateau
かいがん	海岸	beach
ちず	地図	map
きょり	距離	distance
めんせき	面積	area
たかさ	高さ	height

Historical Terms

れきし	歴史	history
れきしてき	歴史的	historical
#せいき	#世紀	#th century
～じだい	～時代	~era/period

Events/Activities

かんこう	観光	sightseeing
かいがいりょこう	海外旅行	overseas trip
キャンプ		camping
まつり	祭	festival

Places in Japan

ほっかいどう	北海道	Hokkaido
ほんしゅう	本州	Honshu
しこく	四国	Shikoku
きゅうしゅう	九州	Kyushu
ちばけん	千葉県	Chiba prefecture (sister state of Wisconsin)
おきなわ	沖縄	Okinawa
さっぽろ	札幌	Sapporo
なごや	名古屋	Nagoya
いせ	伊勢	Ise
よこはま	横浜	Yokohama
にっこう	日光	Nikko
たかやま	高山	Takayama
なら	奈良	Nara
ひろしま	広島	Hiroshima
ながさき	長崎	Nagasaki
おおさか	大阪	Osaka
こうべ	神戸	Kobe
とうきょう	東京	Tokyo
きょうと	京都	Kyoto
ふじさん	富士山	Mt. Fuji
ながの	長野	Nagano

Accommodation

ホテル		hotel
りょかん	旅館	*ryokan* (inn)
みんしゅく	民宿	*minshuku* (bed-and-breakfast-type lodging)

ユースホステル		youth hostel
ホームステイ		homestay
テント		tent

Planning/Preparation

じこくひょう	時刻表	timetable
りょうきん	料金	fare
よてい	予定	plan (schedule)
ようい	用意	preparation/ precaution
じゅんび	準備	preparation
つもり		intention
スーツケース		suitcase

Descriptors

ゆうめい（な）	有名（な）	famous
つくられた	作られた	(to be) made
たてられた	建てられた	(to be) built
できた	出来た	(to be) completed

Verbs

まがる	曲がる	to turn
かえる	買える	to be able to buy
いる	要る	to need
おもう	思う	to think
もっていく	持っていく	to take with (objects)
つれていく	連れていく	to take along (people, pets)
つく	着く	to arrive at
かかる		to take time/cost
たしかめる	確かめる	to make sure
のぼる	登る	to climb
とまる	泊まる	to stay at

Miscellaneous

みやげもの	土産物	souvenir
とくさんひん	特産品	special product

Resources

3

List of Functions and Expressions
General Vocabulary

List of Functions and Expressions

Socializing

Functions	Formal	Less Formal	Structure
Using Different Modes of Speech	山田様 田中先生 太郎さん 恵子さん	山田さん／くん／山田 太郎くん／ちゃん／太郎 恵子ちゃん／恵子	
Greeting	おはようございます。 こんにちは。 こんばんは。 お休みなさい。 おじゃまします／失礼します。 いつも、お世話になっています。 この間は、どうも。	おはよう。 こんにちは。 お休み。	
Talking About Weather	いいお天気ですねえ。 暑いですねえ。 ひどい風（雨、雪）ですねえ。 いやなお天気ですねえ。 今日は、そんなに寒くなかったですね。	いい、天気（だ）ねえ。 暑いねえ。 ひどい風（だ）ねえ。 いやな天気（だ）ねえ。 今日は、そんなに寒くなかったね。	…ねえ Adj (i) stemくなかった
Introducing	山田さんをご紹介します。 こちらは山田さんです。 こちらは西高校の山田さんです。 はじめまして。 山田と申します。 どうぞ　よろしく。 こちらこそ、よろしくお願いします	 山田といいます。 よろしく。 こちらこそ、よろしく。	 ～は～です N の N ～という
Leave-taking	さようなら。 また、今度。 それでは、また。 また、お会いしましょう。 それでは、また、近いうちに。 お元気で。 いってらっしゃい。 いってまいります。 では、気を付けていっていらっしゃい。 がんばってください。	さよなら/バイバイ。 じゃ、また。 また、会いましょう。 じゃ、また、近いうちに。 いってきます。 じゃ、気を付けて。 がんばって。	 ～ましょう ～て ～てください

Functions	Formal	Less Formal	Structure
Leave-taking	失礼します。 お先に、失礼します。 おじゃましました。 お疲れさまでした。 一度、遊びにいらしてください。 どうぞ、お大事に。 お母さんによろしくお伝えください 今後とも、よろしくお願いします。	お先に。 お疲れさま。 一度、遊びに来てください。 お母さんによろしく。 これからも、よろしく。	V に(in order to) お V ください
Thanking	ありがとうございます。 どうも、ありがとうございます。 すみません。 どうも、すみません。 どうも、ありがとうございました。 ありがとうございました。 すみませんでした。 ごちそうさまでした。 いいえ、どういたしまして。 こちらこそ。 お世話になりました。 いい勉強になりました。 おかげさまで。 とても楽しかったです。 お疲れさまでした。	ありがとう。 どうも／ありがとう。 どうも／すみません。 どうも、ありがとう。 ありがとう。 ごちそうさま。 いいえ。 お世話さま。 お疲れさま。	～になる Adj (i) + Nになる Adj (i) stem かった
Agreeing/ Disagreeing	はい／ええ。 はい、（ええ）そうです。 本当に、そうです。 その通りです。 もちろんです。 賛成です。 私もそう思います。 同感です。 さあ、そうかもしれませんね。 そうですねえ。 いいえ。 いいえ、違います。 いいえ、そうではありません。 ちょっと、違うんじゃありませんか。	うん。 うん、そう（だ）よ。 本当に。 そのとおり。 もちろん。 賛成。 私（ぼく）もそう思う。 同感。 さあ、そうかもしれないね そう（だ）ねえ。 ううん。 ううん、違う。 ううん、そうじゃない（わ／ よ）。 ちょっと、違うんじゃない （の／か）。	そう さあ～かもしれない ～ではありません ～んじゃありませんか ／～じゃない

Functions	Formal	Less Formal	Structure
Agreeing/ Disagreeing	そうではないと思いますけど。 それは違うと思います。 そうは思いませんが。 そんなふうには、見えませんが。 さあ、そうでしょうか。	そうじゃないと思うけど。 それは違うと思うな。 そうは思わないけど。 そんなふうには見えないけど さあ、そうかなあ。	〜ないとおもう …な 〜は〜ない …けど …でしょうか / かなあ
Inquiring About Health After a Long Interval	お元気ですか。 お変わりありませんか。 その後、いかがですか。	元気? 変わりない? どう?	
Responding to Questions About Health	はい／ええ、元気です。 はい／ええ、おかげさまで。 はい／ええ、なんとか ちょっと、風邪をひいています。	うん、元気（だ）よ。 うん、おかげさまで。 うん、まあまあ。 ちょっと、風邪ひいている。　〜ています	

Exchanging Information

Functions	Formal	Less Formal	Structure
Identifying Person Identifying Nationality/ Profession	私の名前は、山田恵子です。 15才です。 東京に住んでいます。 私は日本人です。 学校の先生です。 母は英語の教師をしています。 お国はどちらですか。 どちらの方ですか。 日本の方ですか。	〜は〜です 15才（だ）よ。 私（ぼく）は 日本人（だ）よ。 学校の先生 (だ) よ。 国はどこ? どこの人? 日本の人?	#さい 〜ています／〜ている N の N です／だ occupation をして いる
Asking for/ Giving Information	これは何ですか。 これはいくらですか。 一つ、いくらですか。 全部でいくらになりますか。 今、何時ですか。 何時から何時までですか。 何時に始まりますか。 何時に終わりますか。 何時までに行けばいいですか。 どこですか。 どこにありますか。 どこにいますか。 どこへ行きますか。 どこで売っていますか。 どこから来ますか。 どこまで行きますか。 それはどこのカメラですか。 どれですか。 どちら（どっち）ですか。 どの本ですか。 いつですか。 いつからですか。 いつまでですか。 いつ来ますか。	これ、なあに? これ、いくら? 一つ、いくら? 全部でいくら? 今、何時? 何時から何時まで? 何時に始まる? 何時に終わる? 何時までにいけばいい／いいの? どこ? どこにある / あるの? どこにいる / いるの? どこへ行くの? どこで売ってる / 売ってるの? どこから来る / 来るの? どこまで行く / 行くの? それ、どこのカメラ? どれ? どっち / どっちなの? どの本? いつ / いつなの? いつから? いつまで? いつ、来る / 来るの?	〜は〜ですか ひとつ、ふたつ… で (totalizing) time から time まで time に time に time までに どこ place に　ある place に　いる place へ place で どこから どこまで どこの〜 どれ どちら／どっち どの〜 いつ いつから いつまで いつ

Functions	Formal	Less Formal	Structure
Asking for/ Giving Information	どなた／だれですか。 何という人ですか。 だれのですか。 だれが行きますか。 だれと行きますか。 だれに上げましたか。 だれに貰いましたか。 だれを呼びますか。 どうやって行きますか。 何で行きますか。 どう行ったらいいですか。 どう行けばいいですか。 どのくらいかかりますか。 なぜですか。 どうしてですか。 どういう訳ですか。 どういう意味ですか。 それは何のためですか。 それは何といいますか。 英語で何といいますか。 何で出来ていますか。	だれ / どなた? 何ていう人 / 人なの? だれの? だれが行く / 行くの? だれと行く / 行くの? だれに上げた / 上げたの? だれに貰った / 貰ったの? だれを呼ぶ / 呼ぶの? どうやって行く / 行くの? 何で行く / 行くの? どう行ったらいい / いいの? どう行けばいい / いいの? どのくらいかかる / かかるの? なぜ / なんで? どうして? どういう訳? どういう意味? それって、何のため? それ、何ていう / いうの? 英語で何ていう / いうの? 何で出来ている / 出来ているの?	だれ、どなた ～というN だれの だれが ～と(with) person にあげる person にもらう だれを どうやって ～で (by means of) ～たら ～ば どのくらい なぜ どうして どういう（わけ） どういう～ ～のため ～という ～で (by means of) ～で (made of)
Describing People (Physical Traits/ Temperament /Attire)	恵子さんは可愛いです。 あの子は可愛くないです。 恵子さんは背が高いです。 太郎くんは大きい目をしています。 髪を長くしています。 トムくんは金髪です。 スポーツ刈りにしています。 太っています。 背が高くて痩せています。 太郎は元気な子供です。 おばあさんは子供っぽい人です。 太郎は子供らしい子供です。 リサさんはモデルのような人です。	 リサさんはモデルみたいな人です。	～はAdjです ～はAdj (i) stem く ない ～は～がAdj (i) ～はAdj + N (part of body) をしている Adj (i)くしている ～は～です ～にしている ～ている (state) Adj (i) stem くて Adj (na) + N ～ぽい ～らしい ～ような／～みたいな

Functions	Formal	Less Formal	Structure
Describing People (Physical Traits/ Temperament /Attire)	恵子さんは、赤いセーターを着ています。 赤いセーターを着ている人が恵子さんです。		〜ている Relative clause + N
Describing How Things Are	映画は面白かったです。 楽しいパーティーでした。 静かなホテルです。		Adj (i) stem かった Adj (i) + N Adj (na) + N
Asking About and Telling Physical Conditions	お元気ですか。 どうしたんですか。 その後、いかがですか。 お変わりありませんか。 お体の調子は、いかがですか。 あまり、調子がよくないんです。 具合はどうですか。 お陰さまですっかり、よくなりました。 もう、なおりました。 風邪をひいています。 頭(おなか／歯)が痛いんです。 熱があります。 気持ちが悪いんです。 吐き気（頭痛／寒気）がします。 怪我をしました。 咳がでます。 おばあさんが病気になりました。 捻挫（骨折）しました。 おじさんがコレラにかかりました。	元気? どうしたの? その後、どう? 変わりない? 〜になる/なった	どう（する） いかが／どう Adj (i) stem くない Adj (i) stem くなる もう… name of illness に かかる
Expressing One's Own Feelings	私は嬉しい（悲しい）です。 かわいそうですねえ。 パーティーはたのしかったです。 腹が立ちますねえ。 残念です。 私は妹が可愛いです。	わあ、かわいそう! 腹が立つねえ	〜はAdj (i) です Adj (na) です／だ
Expressing the Feelings of Others	あの人は嬉しそうです。 あの人は嬉しいようです。 あの人は悲しんでいます。 あの人は寂しがっています。 あの人は悲しいといっています。		Adj (i) stem そう Adj (i) よう 〜ている Adj (i) stem がる …といっている

Functions	Formal	Less Formal	Structure
Narrating Personal Experiences	子どもの時長野に行きました。 長野に行った時、温泉に入りました。 スキーをしたり、温泉に入ったりしました。 ポップコーンを食べながら、映画を見ました。 長野に行って、スキーをして、温泉に入りました。 長野では、スキーをしてから、温泉に入りました。 スキーをしないで温泉に入りました。 温泉に入る前にスキーをしました。 スキーをしたあとで、温泉に入りました。 富士山に、登ったことがあります。 その映画は、まだ見ていません。 一年間、アメリカに住んでいました。 どんな味がするか、食べてみました。		〜のとき 〜たとき 〜たり〜たりする 〜ながら、 〜て、〜て、 〜てから 〜ないで 〜るまえに 〜たあとで 〜たことがある まだ〜ていない #ねんかん 〜てみる
Inquiring About or Expressing Knowledge	漢字をいくつ知っていますか。 山田さんをご存じですか。 そのお祭のことを知っていますか。 山田さんのことは知りません。 そのことならよくわかっています。 これは、何かわか		〜をいくつ 〜のこと 〜なら なにか
Inquiring About or Expressing Opinions	どう思いますか。 どうお考えですか。 このことについて、意見を言ってください。 ご意見を伺わせてください。 はっきり言って、あまり面白くないと思います。 その意見に賛成です。 わたしは反対です。 あまりよくないような気がします。 この方がいいんではないかと思うんですけど。 この方が、いいんではないでしょうか。	どう思う? この方がいいんじゃないかと思うんだけど。 この方が、いいんじゃない?	どう おVですか。 〜について うかがわせる/きかせる あまり〜ない 〜とおもう 〜ようなきがする 〜ほうが 〜ないかとおもう 〜ないでしょうか
Stating Need	バスに乗るには切符が要ります。 どうしても、お金が必要です。 切符がないと困ります。 朝はコーヒーを飲まずにはいられません。		〜には どうしても 〜ないと 〜ずにはいられない

Functions	Formal	Less Formal	Structure
Inquiring About or Expressing Likes/ Dislikes/ Preferences	恵子さんはケーキが好きですか。 ケーキとクッキーと、どっちが好きですか。 ケーキの方が好きです。 クッキーの方がいいです。 ケーキよりクッキーの方が好きです。 クッキーはあんまり好きではありません。		～は～がすき AとBとどっちが ～のほう ～のほうがいい ～より～のほう ～は～ない
Inquiring About or Expressing Likes/ Dislikes/ Preferences	甘いものは嫌いです。 果物とケーキとクッキーとではどれが一番好きですか。 お菓子の中で、何が一番好きですか。 クッキーはケーキほど好きではありません。 クッキーはケーキよりおいしいと思います。 映画を見るのとスポーツをするのとどっちがいいと思いますか。 お酒を飲むことは好ましくないと思います。 激しいスポーツは好みません。		～と～と～とでは ～がいちばん ～のなかで ～ほど ～ない ～は～より ～の ～とおもう ～ないとおもう
Inquiring About or Expressing Wishes/ Wants/Desires In Others	何か欲しいものがありますか。 私はケーキが食べたいです。 僕は電話をかけたいです。 休みにはハワイへ行きたいです。 新しい車が欲しいです。 将来、先生になりたいです。 いつか、宇宙へ行きたいです。		なにか ～は～が／を～たい time には place へ ほしい ～になりたい いつか
Inquiring About or Expressing Wishes/ Wants/Desires In Others	あの人は行きたがっていますか。 あの人は行きたいと言っていますか。 あの人は行きたいそうです。 あの人は行きたいらしいです。 あの人は行きたいようです。 あの人は車を欲しがっています。		～たがっている ～たいといっている ～たいそうです ～たいらしい ～たいようです ほしがっている
Reporting Something Said	あの人は行くと言っています。 あの人も行くそうです。 あの人も行くんですって。 天気予報によると、雨だそうです。 ひどい映画だと聞いています。 とてもいいという評判です。 とても古いホテルだといわれています。	あの人は行くって。	～といっている ～そうだ …って ～によると…だそうだ …ときいている …というひょうばん …といわれている

Getting Things Done

Functions	Formal	Less Formal	Structure
Requesting	お願いします。 ケーキ、ありますか。 ケーキを下さい。 大きいのを下さい。 静かにしてください。 それを見せてください。 これ見せてくださいませんか。 伝えていただきたいんですが。 明日までに洗っておいてください。 作文を見ていただけますか。 配達を頼みたいんですが。 電話をかけてほしいんです。	ケーキ、ある? ケーキちょうだい／くれ。 静かに。 それ、見せて。 これ見せてくれませんか／くれない（か）。 伝えてもらいたいんですが。 作文を見てもらえますか。 配達を頼みたいんだけど。 ～てほしい	～をください Adj (i)の Adj (na)にする ～てください ～てくださる／～てくれる ～ていただく／～てもらう ～までに、～ておく ～ていただける／～てもらえる ～たいんですが／～たいんだけど
Making Arrangements and Suggestions	何時にしましょうか。 十時はどうですか。 あの店に行ってみましょうか。 あの人に頼みましょう。 あの人に頼んだらどうですか。 自分でやればいいでしょう。	何時にしようか。 十時はどう（かな）。 あの店に行ってみようか。 あの人に頼もう。 あの人に頼んだらどう（かな）。 自分でやれば。	～にする ～はどう ～てみる ～ましょう ～たら　どう ～ばいい
Inviting	いっしょに、行きませんか。 ごいっしょに、いかがですか。 もしよかったら、いらっしゃいませんか。 ぜひ、いらしてください。	いっしょに行かない（か）。 いっしょにどう? よかったら行きませんか／行かない（か）。 ぜひ、来てください。	～ませんか／～ないか Adj (i) stem かったら ～てください
Offering/ Accepting Food and Beverages	お茶をどうぞ。 ジュース、飲みませんか。 どうぞ、召し上がってください。 お茶か何か、いかがですか。 何か冷たいものでもいかがですか。	お茶をどうぞ。 ジュース、飲まない? どうぞ、食べて／飲んでください。 お茶か何かどうですか。 何か冷たいものでもどうですか。	～ませんか／～ないか ～てください ～かなにか ～でも

Functions	Formal	Less Formal	Structure
Offering/ Accepting Food and Beverages	どうも、すみません。 ええ、ありがとうございます。 ええ、いただきます。 では、遠慮なく、いただきます。 どうぞ、お構いなく。	どうも／すみません。 ありがとう。 じゃ、遠慮なく。	
Instructing/ Directing Others to Do Something	この道を、まっすぐ行ってください。 赤いペンで書きます。 遊んでいないで、早く宿題をしなさい。 学校へ行くとき、この手紙を出してください。 先ず初めによく読んで、次に答えを選んで、最後に番号を書いてください。 これは、そのままにしておいてください。 宿題はすぐやることになっています。 辞書は、見ないようにしましょう。 妹に早く帰るようにいってください。 今日は、早く帰るようにしてください。		placeをV 〜で (by means of) 〜ないで 〜なさい …とき まずはじめに… つぎに… さいごに… 〜のままにしておく 〜ことになっている 〜ないようにする 〜ようにいう 〜ようにする

Expressing Attitudes

Functions	Formal	Less Formal	Structure
Expressing Admiration	すごいですねえ。 可愛い靴ですねえ。 よくわかりましたねえ。 山田さんにはとてもかないません。 日本語がじょうずですねえ。 豪華なホテルですねえ。 千字も漢字が書けるんですね。 そんなことは、大人でも出来ません。	すごいねえ／なあ。 可愛い靴（だ）ねえ。 よくわかったねえ。 山田さんにはとてもかなわない（わ／よ）。 日本語がじょうず（だ）ねえ。 千字も漢字が書けるのね／んだね。 〜でも	Adj (i) ねえ／なあ Adj (i) + N よく とても…ない …ねえ。 Adj (na) + N #も
Expressing Interest/ Disinterest	面白そうですね。 富士山には、一度登ってみたいです。 登山に、興味／関心がありますか。 ちょっと、興味があります。 全く、無関心です。		Adj (i) stem そう 〜てみたい 〜にきょうみ／かんしんがある／ない む (prefix)
Expressing Regret	残念でしたね。 お気の毒ですねえ。 それは、いけませんねえ。 大変でしたねえ。 早く行けばよかったです。 もっと勉強するべきでした。 あ、バスが行ってしまいました。 試合に負けてしまいました。 もっと頑張るんでした。 満点のはずでしたのに。	残念だったわね／ね。 気の毒（だ）ねえ。 大変だったわねえ／ねえ。 あ、バスが行っちゃった。 試合に負けちゃった。 もっと頑張るんだった。 満点のはずだったのに。	…ね 〜ば 〜べき 〜てしまう（ちゃう） …のはず、…のに
Expressing Apology	すみません。 遅くなって、すみません。 ごめんなさい。 どうもすみませんでした。 申し訳ありませんでした。 もう、しません。		〜て (reason) もう〜ない

Functions	Formal	Less Formal	Structure
Expressing Apology	私が悪かったんです。 悪いと思っています。 ご迷惑をおかけしました。 みんな私のせいです。 全て私の責任です。		Adj (i) stemかった 〜ている おV する 〜のせい
Expressing Wishes	頑張ってください。 早く良くなりますように。 早く良くなるといいですね。 今日がお正月だったらよかったですね。	頑張ってね。 早く良くなるといいね。 早くお正月になればいいのに。 今日がお正月だったらよかったなあ。	 …ように 〜と …のに 〜だったら …なあ
Reacting to Offers, Requests, Suggestions, Invitations	ありがとうございます。 ぜひ、お願いします。 お世話おかけします。 大丈夫です。 自分で出来ます。 はい、わかりました。 はい。すぐやります。 はい。かしこまりました。 ええと、少し待っていただけますか。 すみません、ちょっと時間がかかるんですが。 木曜日なら、あいています。 それは、いいですねえ。 どちらでもいいです。 私は、かまいませんけど。 ぜひ、伺います。 お世話になります。 残念ですけど。 せっかくですが、水曜日はちょっと。 ちょっと、都合が悪いんですけど。 テスト勉強しなきゃならないので。 折角誘っていただいたのに、申し訳ありませんが。 ぜひ、伺いたいんですが、実は、 ちょっと、予定が入ってしまって。 実は、親と出かけることになっていますので。 また、いつかほかの機会に。	ありがとう。 ぜひ、お願い（頼む）。 うん、わかった。 うん、すぐやる(わ／よ)。 ええと、少し待ってもらえますか。 ちょっと時間がかかるんだけど。 それはいいねえ。 どっちでもいいよ。 私／ぼくはかまわないけど。 残念だけど。 せっかくだけど、水曜日はちょっと。 ちょっと、都合が悪いんだけど。 〜なきゃならない 折角誘ってもらったのに、悪いんだけど。 ぜひ行きたいんだけど、実は、ちょっと、予定が入っちゃって。 実は、親と出かけることになっているので…。	 …んですが／…んだけど 〜なら どちらでも ぜひ 〜になる …けど …が／…けど …んですけど／…んだけど。 〜ていただく／〜てもらう じつは… 〜てしまう／〜ちゃう 〜ことになっている …ので いつか

161

Functions	Formal	Less Formal	Structure
Expressing Degree of Certainty	明日は、雨かもしれません。 たぶん、いい天気になるでしょう。		〜かもしれない たぶん…でしょう／だろう
Expressing Degree of Certainty	私も行くことになるだろうと思います。 行けるかどうかわかりません。 あの人は、来るかもしれないし、来ないかもしれません。 来るか、来ないかわかりません。		〜ことになる 〜かどうか …し、… …か…か

Organizing and Maintaining Communication

Functions	Formal	Less Formal	Structure
Attracting Attention	あのう。 あのう、ちょっと。 ちょっと、すみません。 ごめんください。 お願いします。 ちょっと、伺いますが。		…が
Expressing Comprehension	はい、わかりました。 ああ、そうですか。 なるほど。 やはりそうですか。	うん、わかった。 ああ、そう。 ふうん。 ああ、やっぱり。	
Expressing Lack of Comprehension	えっ。 わかりません。 えっ、何ですか。 ちょっと、待って下さい。 すみません。 よく分からないんですが。 ゆっくり、お願いします。 えっ、ネコがどうしたんですか。 その意味は何ですか。 それはどういう意味ですか。 よく聞いてもわかりません。	わかんない。 えっ、何? ちょっと、待って。 すみません。 よくわからないんだけど。 えっ、ネコがどうしたの? それ、どういう意味?	…んですが／…んだけど ～ても
Asking for Repetition or Rephrasing	えっ? えっ、何ですか。 もう一度お願いします。 もう一度言ってください。 すみません、 それは、どういうことでしょうか。 今何て言いましたか。 今何ておっしゃいましたか。 もう一度おっしゃっていただけますか。 ほかの日本語では、何ですか。 ほかの言い方がありますか。	えっ、何? もう一度、お願い。 もう一度、言って。 今何て言ったの／言った? 今何て言いましたか。いう もう一度言ってもらえますか。 ほかの日本語で何? ほかの言い方、ある?	どういうこと ～て（～と）いう ～とおっしゃる／～という ～ていただける／～てもらえる ほかの

Functions	Formal	Less Formal	Structure
Asking How to Say Something In Japanese	日本語で何ですか。 それは日本語で何といいますか。 日本語でどういいますか。 日本語でどういったらいいですか。	日本語で何? 日本語で何ていうの? 日本語でどういうの? 日本語でどういったらいい?	〜で(by means of) 〜と いう どう 〜たら いい
Asking How to Write Something Mentioned	それは、ひらがな／カタカナ／漢字で どう書きますか。 どう書いたらいいか、教えてください。 その漢字の 書き方を教えてください。 小さい「つ」がありますか。		〜で (by means of) …か、… 〜かた
Asking Someone to Explain What They Said	それは、どういう意味ですか。 よくわかるように、説明していただけませんか。 いま、おっしゃったことが、よくわかりません。 もっと簡単に言ってください。	それって、どういう意味? よくわかるように説明してもらえませんか。 〜たこと	どういう 〜ように Adj (na)に
Inquiring/ Expressing Decision	何にしますか。 私は蕎麦にします。 蕎麦でいいですか。 明日は、うちにいます。 うちにいることにします。	何にする? 私／ぼくは蕎麦にする（わ／よ）。 蕎麦でいい? 明日はうちにいる（わ／よ）。 うちにいることにする（わ／よ）。	〜にする 〜でいい 〜ます 〜ことにする
Expressing Intention	明日は、うちにいようと思います。 明日は、うちにいるつもりです。 おとなになったら先生になるつもりです。 バイクを買うために、アルバイトをします。 その窓は、わざと開けてあるんです。		Vうとおもう 〜つもり 〜になる 〜ために 〜てある
Expressing Capability/ Possibility	私は英語が出来ます。 私は英語が得意です。 フランス語はあまり得意ではありません。 私は英語が話せます。 私は英語を話すことが出来ます。 鍵を忘れて、家に入れませんでした。		〜が できる 〜がとくい Adj (na)ではない はなす／はなせる 〜ことができる はいる／はいれる

164

Functions	Formal	Less Formal	Structure
Expressing Cause/Reason	面白いから好きです。 おいしかったので沢山食べました。 面白そうだから見に行きましょう。 だからそう言ったでしょう。 大雪で道路が閉鎖されました。		…から …ので ～にいく だから ～で (because of)
Expressing Problems	困りましたねえ。 車がないので、困っています。 困ったことになりました。 大きな問題になっています。 困ったものですね。 宿題を忘れてしまったんです。 100円しかありません。 どうしましょう。 それは問題ですね。	困ったねえ 宿題を忘れちゃった（の／ん だ）。 100円しかない。。 どうしよう。 それは問題（だ）ね。	…ので ～になる ～てしまう ～んです／～んだ ～しか…ない
Expressing Complaint	変な臭いがしますね。 こんなに少ないんですか。 まだ、出来ていないんですか。 いくらなんでも、おそ過ぎますよ。 まずいパンですねえ。 雨に降られました。 バスに行かれてしまいました。 むりに甘いものを食べさせられました。 書きにくいペンですねえ。 なんて読みにくい字なんでしょう。	 バスに行かれちゃった。 なんて読みにくい字なんだろう。	Adj (na) + N …んですか まだ…ない ～すぎる Adj (i) + N ふる／ふられる (Passive) Passive + てしまう ～させられる ～にくい なんて…だろう
Expressing Obligation	宿題をしなければなりません。 宿題をしなくてはなりません。 学生はみんな宿題をすることになります。 宿題は、しない訳にはいきません。 嫌だけど、そうせざるをえません。 もっと勉強するべきです。	宿題をしなけりゃ。 宿題をしなくちゃ。	～なければならない ～なくてはならない ～ことになる ～ないわけにはいかない ～せざるをえない ～べき
Giving Advice	早く寝たほうがいいですよ。 そんなことは、しないほうがいいです。 早く寝たら、どうですか。		～たほうがいい ～ないほうがいい ～たらどう

Functions	Formal	Less Formal	Structure
Asking for/ Giving Permission Expressing Approval/ Disapproval	うちへ帰ってもいいでしょうか。 はい／ええ、いいですよ。 ここに座っても、かまいませんか。 ええ、どうぞ。 宿題を出さなくてもいいですか。 うちへ、帰らせてください。 それでいい（結構）です。 だめです。 いけません。 それはちょっと困ります。 とんでもありません。 いいえ、ここで遊ばないでください。 テレビばかり見ていてはだめですよ。 そんなことしてはいけません／だめです。 ここで遊ばないようにしましょう。	うちへ帰ってもいい（かしら／かな）。 うん、いい（わ／よ）。 ここに座ってもいいかな。 それでいいわ／よ。 だめ（よ／だ）。 いけない。 とんでもない。 テレビばかり見ていちゃだめ（だ）よ。 そんなことしちゃいけない／だめだ。 ここで遊ばないようにしよう。	〜てもいい かな／かしら 〜てもかまわない 〜なくてもいい かえる／かえらせる 〜でいい 〜ないでください 〜ばかり 〜てはいけない／だめ 〜ないようにする
Prohibiting	ここで煙草を吸わないでください。 煙草を吸ってはいけません。 漫画を読むな。 立ち入り禁止 禁煙 立ち読みお断り。 かばんを持たずに、学校に来てはいけません。 煙草を吸わないようにしましょう。	ここで煙草を吸わないで。 煙草を吸っちゃだめ。	〜ないでください 〜てはいけない／だめ …な(prohibition) おV stem (command) 〜ずに 〜ないようにする
Expressing Friendship	友達じゃありませんか。 友達でしょう? さすが親友ですね。 道理で気が合うんですね。	友達じゃない（の／か）。 友達でしょう／だろう? さすが親友（だ）ね。 道理で気が合うの／んだね。	
Hypothe-sizing	もし、魔法が使えたらどうしますか。 もし、百万円、当たったとしたら何を買いますか。		もし…たら もし…としたら

General Vocabulary

Numbers

いち	一	1
に	二	2
さん	三	3
し／よん	四	4
ご	五	5
ろく	六	6
しち／なな	七	7
はち	八	8
く／きゅう	九	9
じゅう	十	10
じゅういち	十一	11
じゅうに	十二	12
にじゅう	二十	20
さんじゅう	三十	30
ひゃく	百	100
せん	千	1,000
まん	万	10,000
ひとつ	一つ	one item
ふたつ	二つ	two items
みっつ	三つ	three items
よっつ	四つ	four items
いつつ	五つ	five items
むっつ	六つ	six items
ななつ	七つ	seven items
やっつ	八つ	eight items
ここのつ	九つ	nine items
とお	十	ten items

Counters

こ	個	piece
にん	人	person
ドル		dollar
えん	円	yen
ほん	本	long object
さつ	冊	volume (bound object)
そく	足	footgear
まい	枚	flat object
ど	度	frequency (times)
わ	羽	birds/rabbits
はい	杯	cup/spoon
けん	軒	house
だい	台	vehicles/electronics
とう	頭	big animal
ひき	匹	small animal

Frequency

いつも		always
たいてい		usually
よく		often
ときどき	時々	sometimes
#ど	#度	# times
#かい	#回	# times
まいにち	毎日	everyday
ほとんど. (…ない)		almost never
いちども（…ない）		not even once
すぐ		at once/soon

Time/Duration

#じ	#時	# o'clock
#ふん	#分	# minutes
〜はん	〜半	half past #
#しゅうかん	#週間	# weeks
#かげつ	#カ月	# months
#じかん	#時間	# hours
#ねん	#年	# years
#がつ	#月	name of month
#にち	#日	days of the month
ついたち	一日	first (day of the month)
ふつか	二日	second
みっか	三日	third
よっか	四日	fourth
いつか	五日	fifth
むいか	六日	sixth
なのか	七日	seventh
ようか	八日	eighth
ここのか	九日	ninth
とおか	十日	tenth
はつか	二十日	twentieth
ごぜん	午前	a.m.
ごご	午後	p.m.
ことし	今年	this year
らいねん	来年	next year
きょねん	去年	last year

Month

こんげつ	今月	this month
らいげつ	来月	next month
せんげつ	先月	last month

Week

こんしゅう	今週	this week
らいしゅう	来週	next week
せんしゅう	先週	last week

Days of the Week

〜ようび	〜曜日	~day
にちようび	日曜日	Sunday
げつようび	月曜日	Monday
かようび	火曜日	Tuesday
すいようび	水曜日	Wednesday

168

もくようび	木曜日	Thursday
きんようび	金曜日	Friday
どようび	土曜日	Saturday
きのう	昨日	yesterday
きょう	今日	today
あした	明日	tomorrow
せんじつ	先日	the other day
おととい	一昨日	the day before yesterday
あさって	明後日	the day after tomorrow
～まえ	～前	ago

Ordinal Number

#じかんめ	#時間目	class period (first hour)
#ばんめ	#番目	the #th

Asking for Information

なに（なん～）	What?
どこ	Where?
いくら	How much? (price)
だれ	Who?
いつ	When?
どんな	What kind of? (description)
どうして／なぜ	Why?

Pointing To

これ	this one
それ	that one
あれ	that one (over there)
どれ	which one
このN	this
そのN	that
あのN	that (over there)
どのN	which

Describing How to do an Action

こう	this way
そう	that way
ああ	that way (pointing away or imagining)
どう	how? (what way?)

Vかた	～方	how to~
Nちゅう	～中	in the middle of an action

Sequencing

まず	先ず	first
はじめに		first of all
だいいち	第一	first
つぎに	次に	next
それから		after that
さいごに	最後に	lastly
けつろんとして	結論として	in conclusion
そのあとで	その後で	after that
そのまえに	その前に	before that

Preference

すき	好き	like
きらい	嫌い	dislike

Praising Other's Skill

じょうず	上手	good at/skillful

Expressing Capability/Ability

とくい	得意	good at
じしん	自信	confidence
へた		not good at/unskillful
にがて	苦手	not good at

Expressing Degree of Performance/Preference

かなり		considerably
わりと		fairly
ちょっと		a little
やっぱり		as expected
まだ		not yet
あんまり		not so much

Degree of Prediction

きっと		surely
たぶん		probably

Location

うえ	上	on
した	下	under
なか	中	inside
まえ	前	in front
うしろ	後ろ	at the back
あいだ	間	between
となり	隣	next to
てまえ	手前	before
～がわ	～側	~side (right, left)
そば		near
よこ	横	alongside
#かい	#階	# floor

Direction

みなみ	南	south
きた	北	north
ひがし	東	east
にし	西	west
みぎ	右	right
ひだり	左	left
まっすぐ	真直ぐ	straight
こちら		this way
そちら		that way
あちら		that way (over there)
どちら		which way

Weather

いいてんき	いい天気	good weather
あめ	雨	rainy
はれ	晴れ	sunny

くもり	曇り	cloudy
ゆき	雪	snowy
かぜ	風	windy
たいふう	台風	typhoon
あたたかい	温かい	warm
あつい	暑い	hot
さむい	寒い	cold
すずしい	涼しい	cool

Seasons

はる	春	spring
なつ	夏	summer
あき	秋	autumn
ふゆ	冬	winter

Describing Colors

あかい	赤い	red
あおい	青い	blue
しろい	白い	white
くろい	黒い	black
きいろい	黄色い	yellow
みどりいろ	緑色	green
ちゃいろ	茶色	brown
グレー		gray
ベージュ		beige
オレンジいろ		orange
むらさきいろ	紫色	purple
まっか	真赤	stark red
まっくろ	真黒	pitch black
まっしろ	真白	pure white
こい	濃い	dark
うすい	薄い	pale/light

Descriptors

ひくい	低い	low
たかい	高い	high/expensive/tall
おおきい	大きい	large/tall
ちいさい	小さい	small
ながい	長い	long
みじかい	短い	short
おおい	多い	abundant
すくない	少ない	few/little
ふるい	古い	old
あたらしい	新しい	new
やすい	安い	cheap
ひろい	広い	wide/broad/vast
せまい	狭い	narrow
くらい	暗い	dark
あかるい	明るい	light
たのしい	楽しい	enjoyable
よい（いい）	良い	good
わるい	悪い	bad

Verbs

ある		to be/exist (inanimate)
いる		to be/exist (animate)
いく	行く	to go
くる	来る	to come
かえる	帰る	to return (come back)
まつ	待つ	to wait
たべる	食べる	to eat
のむ	飲む	to drink
よむ	読む	to read
かく	書く	to write
きく	聞く	to hear/listen
みる	見る	to see/watch
はなす	話す	to talk/speak
とる	取る	to take
する		to do/play sports
つかう	使う	to use
たつ	立つ	to stand
すわる	座る	to sit
あるく	歩く	to walk
はしる	走る	to run
いる	要る	to need
おもう	思う	to think
わかる	分かる／解る	to know/understand
しる	知る	to know/be aware of
こたえる	答える	to answer
いう	言う	to say
でる	出る	to go out
はいる	入る	to enter
はじめる	始める	to start
おわる	終わる	to end
きをつける	気を付ける	to be careful